Great Women of Faith

Inspiration for Action

Sue Stanton

ILLUSTRATED BY

Charlie Craig

Paulist Press
New York/Mahwah, N.J.

Cover art and interior illustrations by Charlie Craig

Cover design by Lynn Else

Text copyright © 2003 by Sue Stanton
Illustrations © 2003 by Charlie Craig

Library of Congress Cataloging-in-Publication Data

Stanton, Sue, 1952-
    Great women of faith : inspiration for action / Sue Stanton ; illustrated by Charles Craig.
        p. cm.
    Summary: Presents biographies of women from a variety of backgrounds and circumstances who heard a call from God and answered, some by actions that brought international attention and some in the quiet of a cloister.
    Includes bibliographical references.
    ISBN 0-8091-4123-X (alk. paper)
    1. Catholic women—Biography—Juvenile literature. [1. Catholic Church—Biography. 2. Women—Biography.] I. Craig, Charles, 1974- ill. II. Title.
    BX4667.S73   2003
    282′.092′2—dc21

                                                            2003003642

Published by Paulist Press
997 Macarthur Boulevard
Mahwah, New Jersey 07430

www.paulistpress.com

Printed and bound in the United States of America

This book is dedicated to my mother,
Bernice Pennington,
who in 1962 showed that she was
a true woman of faith.

Table of Contents

Acknowledgments vii

Introduction ix

Jane Addams 1

Josephine Bakhita 4

Thea Bowman 7

Mother Frances Cabrini 10

Agneta Chang 13

Frances Crowe 16

Dorothy Day 19

Catherine de Hueck Doherty 22

Mother Katharine Drexel 26

Maria Faustina 29

Maria Goretti 32

José Hobday 34

Juana Inés de la Cruz 37

Chiara Lubich 40

Mother Mary MacKillop 44

Raïssa Maritain 48

Zelie Martin 51

Mary of the Incarnation 54

Flannery O'Connor .57

Maura O'Halloran 60

Contents

Rosa Parks 63

Helen Prejean 66

Mollie Rogers 69

Elaine Roulet 72

Elizabeth Ann Seton .75

Mother Maria Skobtsova 78

Edith Stein 81

Kateri Tekakwitha 84

Mother Teresa 87

Teresa of Avila 90

Thérèse of Lisieux 93

Sojourner Truth 97

Simone Weil 100

Lois Wilson 103

Additional References 106

Acknowledgments

The author would like to extend her appreciation for the assistance in the completion of this work to the following: Father Howard Hansen, O.F.M. Conv.; Father Terry Rasmussen, O.F.M. Conv.; Father Dismas Veeneman, O.F.M. Conv.; Dr. Mary Sawyer; Jo Anne Dalhoff; and Sister Martha Bourne. To Regina da Silva for a lovely conversation, to Anton Nassar for endless hours of Internet help, and to my husband for his patient listening.

And to the one who helps me every day in many ways, Anne Recker—my heartfelt thanks.

Introduction

One of my most striking childhood memories is that of walking behind my mother. I can still see her—her spine straight, her chin lifted slightly, her white purse swaying back and forth, back and forth, dangling from her left elbow. A pair of immaculate white gloves covered her hands and contrasted sharply with the staccato clicking of high-heeled shoes hitting pavement.

Behind this southern lady marched a handful of other mothers, seventy-five schoolchildren, and myself. We followed her down a busy two-lane highway known as U.S. Highway 42, which traversed the state of Kentucky from its northernmost borders down its western side. As the leader of a protest march that came to be known in Kentucky history as The Marching Mothers of Boone County, my mother never complained about her feet or about the shouts and jeers from the owners of vehicles that threatened to hit her as she walked at the head of the line.

A housewife with two children, she was now a woman with a mission. It was 1961, and Catholic school children had been suddenly thrown off the public school buses on which they had ridden for years. Issues of separation of church and state were involved, or so the complainants lodged. But while the issues were argued, what were the children to do? How would they get to school? No one listened to the voices of the Catholic mothers whose children had no form of transportation. No one cared that much for Catholic children in a largely Protestant county.

The protest took Boone County and Kentucky by surprise. Catholics in Kentucky had never been much of a problem before and could easily be dealt with. A few years earlier, a diocesan priest named Father Paul Ciangetti had wanted to start a new parish and build a small church. When news of this got out, it was greeted by sticks of dynamite and a note that read, "Next time, these'll be lit."

But when children became pawns in this game of hatred, my mother decided the bigotry had gone far enough. She and a circle of her friends decided to march the children along the highway their bus traveled, two miles to school each day, two miles back. Their hope was to raise the public's awareness and to be given the right to pay for the use of the bus.

It was in this atmosphere of hatred and intolerance that we walked the highway every day during the school year from 1961–62. It was also a time when one of the largest construction projects the United States had ever built, the interstate highway system, had begun as well.

We marched in single file, stretched out in a line along the highway, carrying our signs with slogans of "TAXATION WITHOUT TRANSPORTATION" and "CHILDREN'S LIVES ARE IN DANGER." To avoid earthmovers and bulldozers, we had to walk a longer route down a hill where they had already churned up clay chunks as large as boulders. When it rained, we sank into wet mud up to our ankles. When it snowed, we slipped and slid on the icy clay. I would arrive at school most days with shoes caked with thick, cold mud and my socks yellow. They took the entire day to dry, only to be put on for the march back home again. Throughout the entire school year—fall, winter, and spring—this was our routine. Finally, after my mother had received hate mail and bomb threats, and had paid for two more pairs of shoes, political negotiations broke the deadlock and we were allowed to now pay to ride the bus once again.

There are times in our lives in which the right thing to do is presented to us. Do we follow the call, or do we hide under the bed until the urge passes? How do we even know when we are called? And whether it's the right call? Does it need to be a trumpet blast, or do we hear the still, small voice? Perhaps we feel that only saints are called to do great things. But if we believe that we are all to be considered saints, then what excuse can we give?

The following biographies are of women who all heard the voice of God and answered. These women came from a wide variety of circumstances and backgrounds with no special preparation or qualification except for a willingness to listen to and answer that call. Sometimes the vision before them was great; sometimes it was small. Sometimes their response was directed outward into the world; sometimes it was an inner, contemplative response. Many times they responded to the call with feelings of disbelief and doubt. That's when prayer and faith were the only things left for each to hold onto.

These women of faith have laid new ground for us to dig our own roots deep into. They surround us, surprise us, and have ignited the world we live in. May each one of them burn as a flame through the darkness of time and become a torch of light that is passed down from one outstretched hand to the next.

Jane Addams

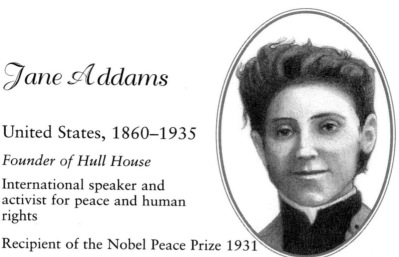

United States, 1860–1935

Founder of Hull House

International speaker and
activist for peace and human
rights

Recipient of the Nobel Peace Prize 1931

*"Nothing could be worse than the fear that one
had given up too soon...."*

Little Jane Addams sat in the parlor of her Illinois
home, listening. Her father John was a state senator, and he
was having yet another political discussion with President
Abraham Lincoln. They talked about many of society's problems—class struggles, poverty, the desperate life of war wid-
ows and orphans. Listening to their dialogue triggered a
restless feeling in Jane, though it would be many years before
she'd be able to take on the arena of "a man's world" and the
problems within it.

After attending Rockford College in 1882, Jane set out
on a world tour. Of all the sights she saw, none was more
compelling than the poverty of England and the attempt
being made there to combat it. Newly opened Toynbee Hall

in London was a social experiment that ignited her imagination. At Toynbee Hall, the most privileged members of society paid to live among the poor, to teach and be taught by them. Jane decided to return to Chicago and, with a group of like-minded women, set about opening up a center similar in goals.

Chicago in the late 1800s was a city teaming with immigrants from all over the world. How would they fit in American society yet keep their own cultural ways? Jane was determined to welcome these new neighbors and to help them become more involved with American society while obtaining a better life for themselves and their children.

She opened an old mansion and called it Hull House after its previous owner. It became a hub of activity where classes were given on art, music, education, and drama. She encouraged neighboring immigrants to bring and display their cultural symbols and ideas so that an exchange could take place between the older established American class and the newly arrived.

But even after Hull House had begun its journey to what is now called the field of social work, Jane did not stop there. She became involved with such political issues as women's rights, housing and sanitation efforts, legal protection for immigrants, and child labor laws. She laid much of the groundwork for the establishment of the juvenile court system. And with the start of World War I, she expanded her efforts and led international campaigns for peace.

It was not until the end of her life that one could see how much her father and his friend Abraham Lincoln had influenced her. The little girl who listened to their discussions had learned her lessons and pursued her goals with persistence.

"Nothing could be worse," she said, "than the fear that one had given up too soon, and left one unexpended effort that might have saved the world."

For Further Reading

Twenty Years at Hull House by Jane Addams (New York: Signet, 1999).

Josephine Bakhita

Sudan, 1869–1947

Kidnapped as a child and made a slave

Member of the Daughters
of Charity

First saint of the Sudan

"The Lord has loved me so much...."

A woman entered the room carrying a dish of flour, a dish of salt, and a razor. Bakhita eyed her fearfully as the stranger marked her skin with strange patterns. Then the woman picked up the razor. The teenaged Bakhita desperately wanted to run but she couldn't. She was a slave, and her master stood right behind her with a whip.

As a girl she'd been happy, living in a village in the Sudan. Her family was influential and wealthy. Life was secure. *She* was secure. All that changed the day she was kidnapped, stolen by slave traders. They changed the nine-year-old girl's name to Bakhita, meaning "the fortunate one." Perhaps the name had been meant as a cruel joke, but ultimately she agreed she had been most fortunate.

Bakhita was bought and sold repeatedly, each time moving farther and farther away from her family and everything she knew. Finally she was bought by a Turkish general and taken to his house to work. Years later, she spoke of the torture that she endured there, a type of tattooing by use of scars instead of ink. A pattern was marked, then cut into the skin with a razor. Salt was poured into the wound to make the scar more visible.

"My face was spared," she said, "but six patterns were designed on my breasts, and sixty more on my belly and arms. I thought I would die, especially when salt was poured in the wounds....It was by a miracle of God I didn't die. He had destined me for better things."

In 1885 Bakhita was given to the Italian consul as a gift. She traveled to Italy where she became a nurse to his daughter. Accompanying the girl to boarding school, Bakhita became acquainted with the Canossian sisters and heard the gospel message of freedom. Soon the consul had to return to the Sudan and planned to take both his daughter and Bakhita back with him. Bakhita wished to remain behind. With the help of the sisters she discovered that slavery was illegal in Italy and therefore she was already free. She decided to be baptized and a few years later entered the Canossian order and became a religious.

For over fifty years, Sister Josephine Bakhita served her order well. She was known for her generous nature and wit, and later for her extraordinary holiness. Always the helper, she served the other sisters and forgave all the horrors that had been imposed on her in the past. "If I were to meet the slave traders who kidnapped me and even those who tortured me," she said, "I would kneel and kiss their hands, for if that did not happen, I would not be a Christian and religious today...."

Perhaps of all the extraordinary events of her life, Sister Josephine Bakhita's attitude of forgiveness is the most remarkable.

For Further Reading

"Blessed Josephine Bakhita" in *All Saints* by Robert Ellsberg (New York: Crossroad, 1997).

Thea Bowman

United States, 1937–1990

Convert to Catholicism

Franciscan sister of Perpetual Adoration

Singer, teacher, international speaker on African American culture

"If we are not family, we can't become Church."

Little Bertha Bowman sat in class listening to the black-clad figure in front of her. She was spellbound by the story she heard. Never good at math, she realized that she could be good at reading, something she had never thought possible after attending a public school for five years.

Her mother had taken her out of public school to give Bertha a better education. In the 1940s, public education in Mississippi was poor for everyone, and for African American children even worse. If the sisters hadn't arrived and opened the Holy Child Jesus School in Canton, Bertha might never have known what she was truly capable of.

"I was good in reading, so I had to help someone else. We didn't realize it, but we were learning to cooperate and to build our community," she would say years later.

When Bertha was ten, she shocked her Episcopalian family by announcing that she wanted to become a Catholic. When she was a high school junior, she shocked them again by telling them that she wanted to be a nun. Her father warned her, "They are not going to like you up there, the only black in the middle of all the whites." Her reply was typical: "I'm going to make them like me."

Bertha became Sister Thea, which means "of God." Her life as a religious put her on a path that would lead her back to Mississippi, teaching and preaching and singing.

Sister Thea never forgot how it felt to be the only African American in an all-white church. But instead of blending in, she decided to point it out. She knew that only by being herself could she really be of benefit to the people of God, and she was a person of color. She wanted to make other people of color feel as comfortable in the church as she felt.

"What does it mean to be black and Catholic?" she would ask the crowds she spoke to. "It means that I come to my church fully functioning. That doesn't frighten you, does it?" She challenged African American Catholics to become involved with the church in every way.

She shared the joy of her heritage through her singing, dancing, and cultural traditions. Using her music, her personal history, and the history of African Americans, she brought pride to them while increasing the awareness of the larger church. She encouraged all people to join in the joy of the love of God and to share that joy and love even through hardship.

Despite having breast cancer for over six years, Sister Thea kept up her rounds of public singing and preaching until the end of her life. Many times she performed from her wheelchair and in great pain. But the beauty of God shone through her. She prayed that "I live 'til I die."

Today the fruits of her work permeate our society. Health care centers, houses for the homeless, gospel choirs all named in her honor speak to thousands daily of the joy-giving spark that Sister Thea Bowman was for humankind.

For Further Reading

Sister Thea Bowman, Shooting Star: Selected Writings and Speeches, edited by Celestine Cepress (Winona, Minn.: St. Mary's Press, 1993).

Sister Thea: Her Own Story, a video recording (St. Louis: Oblate Media and Communications Corp., 1991).

Mother Frances Cabrini

Italy, 1850–1917

Founder of the Missionaries of the Sacred Heart

Missionary to Italian immigrants in the United States

Founded numerous schools, hospitals, orphanages, and convents

"For God it is not the possible we should do, but the impossible."

When Francesca Cabrini was born, she was small and fragile, the last of thirteen children born to a farmer in nineteenth-century Italy. Only four of the children survived, and surprisingly this tiny infant was one of them. Francesca's frailty was to follow her all her life. But only those who did not know her underestimated her because of her physical limitations. Her spiritual strength enabled her to perform extraordinary labors. "The weak things of this world God has chosen to shame the strong," she said, echoing St. Paul.

Francesca wanted to become a missionary to China but was twice rejected by convents due to her poor health. Instead she worked on the family farm after her parents died. Then a priest asked her to help a local community that was taking care of children at an orphanage. The assignment was to last two weeks. It lasted over two years.

At the request of a bishop, Francesca left the assignment to form a new society for women. She was finally not only being accepted as a member of a religious community, but she was also to be its superior! She named her community the Missionaries of the Sacred Heart, still hoping that God was calling her to be a missionary to China.

But Pope Leo XIII had other ideas for Francesca, who was now known as Mother Cabrini. In the later part of the nineteenth century, Italian immigrants were flooding into the United States. Help for them in their new home was desperately needed, he explained. He wanted her to go to America.

Mother Cabrini agreed and took several sisters with her. Crossing the Atlantic in 1889 proved just how necessary her presence was in the new country. Most of the fifteen hundred passengers aboard the ship became ill. Her sisters nursed the people while teaching them about God's love. As a result, many of the sisters became ill as well. Mother Cabrini herself fell sick but continued to work. She wanted to educate these people who would soon be in a brand new country, neither knowing the language nor having jobs waiting for them.

On March 31, 1889, the boat entered New York Harbor, but Mother's problems were only beginning. Her largest obstacles came from the church itself. First, there was no one even to meet them at the dock. Then they learned that the archbishop of New York had changed his mind and no longer wanted them. There was no place to stay, no food, no money, and no way of getting any help from the church that had asked them to come. The archbishop had problems enough, he said; they would have to solve their own.

The sisters went door to door and begged.

They begged for food, for money, and for shelter that they might start an orphanage. They received all these things and more. A wealthy Italian woman, the Contessa di Cesnola, became their sponsor and provided the house and means for the sisters to start their orphanage for poor Italian children.

Mother Cabrini helped Italian immigrants settle into a new land that was often angry at the number of strangers pouring into the country by the millions. The immigrants brought new customs and new ways of looking at life, ways so foreign to Americans that racist attitudes resulted. But neither racism nor the ongoing lack of support from the church kept Mother Cabrini from pursuing her simple vision: to bring to those immigrating and emigrating the tools they needed to adapt to their changing environments.

In later years, she suffered further ill health but still managed to travel extensively and to found over fifty orphanages, hospitals, schools, and houses of her religious community in many different countries. She said, "The whole world is not wide enough for me." Nine years after her death, a branch of her community was established in China, fulfilling at last her lifelong dream.

Mother Cabrini became an American citizen a few years before her death. When she was canonized, she became the first American saint.

For Further Reading

American Women of Faith by Rawley Myers (Huntington, Ind.: Our Sunday Visitor, 1989).

ℐgneta Chang

Korea, 1906–1950

*Maryknoll sister, teacher,
and missionary*

Social activist

Kidnapped and murdered by
North Korean Communists

"...To help my country and my people."

Mary Chang always wanted to be a religious. Her family, politically prominent in Korea, was very proud that her two older brothers had become priests. Mary chose to follow them into the religious life by becoming a Maryknoll sister. This newly formed American order was devoted to missionary action around the world, including Mary's homeland of Korea. The Maryknoll sisters welcomed the sixteen-year-old girl and flew her to America for training at their motherhouse in New York State. When they asked her why she wanted to be a religious, her answer was simple: "In order to become holy and then to help my country and people."

When her religious training had ended, Mary returned home with the new name of Sister Agneta. For many years she served in parishes, teaching the children who were impoverished by Korea's frequent changes in government. When

World War II broke out, the country was invaded by the Japanese. Rather than leave when the American Maryknolls were forced out, Sister Agneta stayed behind to start the first community of Korean sisters. The war cut her off not only from her order but from news of the world. After the war ended, Korea was effectively divided in two as part of the peace agreement. Sister Agneta and her group of inexperienced sisters were trapped in the north in what was now the Russian-Communist–occupied half.

When the Russians left Northern Korea in 1949, the Korean Communists gained control. Very anti-Catholic, they began a "cleansing" of religious orders, which meant disbanding the groups and killing its members. Special targets were those priests and religious of prominence, such as Sister Agneta and her brothers. She and one other sister fled for protection to a nearby Catholic village.

A decree was sent to every village demanding that everyone report for work duty. Sister Agneta was unable to comply. Suffering for many years with a back injury, she could not get out of bed to walk to the reporting place. In constant pain, she lay waiting for what would happen next. Soldiers came looking for her.

The villagers were forced to place Sister Agneta on the floor of a bare wooden ox cart. They could hear both her cries of pain and her prayers as the cart pulled away. No one saw her again. Word came back to the village that Sister Agneta, along with several others, had been shot in the head and left by the side of the road.

As novice mistress, Sister Agneta was instrumental in encouraging vocations in the Korean branch of the Maryknoll sisters. As martyr, her love and service extend far beyond that small country to the world.

For Further Reading

"Agneta Chang" in *All Saints* by Robert Ellsberg (New York: Crossroad, 1997).

Frances Crowe

United States, 1919–

Wife, mother, peace activist

Arrested and jailed over
thirty times

*"There is more opportunity for each of us
to make a difference now than ever before
in human history."*

Frances Crowe had moved to Northampton, Massachu-setts, merely to get the best education possible for her pro-foundly deaf son. She found herself living in an area famous for promoting such social reforms as race equality, education, women's and children's rights, and more. When the atomic bomb was exploded at Hiroshima, Japan, in 1945, Frances found she was not the only one greatly disturbed by the event and its implications. She began what would ultimately become a lifetime of protest.

By the mid 1950s she had joined the Women's International League for Peace and Freedom founded by turn-of-the-century social reformer Jane Addams. In later years Crowe would also join the Society of Friends, or Quakers, whose spiritually based positions on war and peace were a good match for her own.

In the '60s and '70s, it seemed as if the rest of the country had finally caught up. The news was filled with reports, commentaries, and speculations about nuclear war, testing, and treaties. Weapons were being stockpiled for certain future use. Frequent radiation exposure was also a major concern. Exactly how much exposure was too much? What did the threat and reality of nuclear war really mean for the world's children? What should be done?

For Frances Crowe, the answers seemed simple—just get rid of the stuff.

When the 1963 Test Ban Treaty was finally in its formation stages, Crowe joined groups protesting the Vietnam War. She acted as a draft counselor, insisting that young men either enter the service or object to it with informed thinking, having sorted out moral and political questions. After the pullout from Vietnam, Crowe extended her efforts to curbing the nuclear arms buildup, preventing the development of biological weapons, ending sanctions against the Iraqi people, instituting campaign finance reform, and limiting the power of global corporations.

In 1983 she received the John Leary Award of the New England Catholic Peace Fellowship. That same year, she also accepted the Peace and Justice Award of the United Methodist Southern New England Conference. In accepting the second she said, "There is more opportunity for each of us to make a difference now than ever before in human history."

Crowe's commitment to peace and justice has continued for half a century and included being arrested and jailed more than thirty times. In 1998, at the age of eighty, she and six others were arrested for trespassing at a nuclear weapons plant that made cruise missiles and "smart bombs." That same year she was arrested at an antinuclear protest at a U.S. naval base.

"I have tried for many years to educate myself and my community about the futility of war. I have vigiled, prayed, marched, written letters to the editor, held meetings, and shown films—in other words, organized against the nuclear arms race." But, looking backward, she added, "I see nothing gloomy about acting to stop the end of life on this planet....and we do not have to do it alone. I believe there is a spirit—life force, God—that is helping us every day."

For Further Reading

Justice Seekers, Peace Makers: Thirty-Two Portraits in Courage by Michael True (Mystic, Connecticut: Twenty-Third Publications, 1985).

Dorothy Day

United States, 1897–1980

Mother, writer, convert to Catholicism, social activist

Cofounder of the Catholic Worker movement

"All times are in the hand of God."

Eight-year-old Dorothy lay in bed sleeping on the night of April 18, 1906. The house began to shake, and her bed slid from one end of the room to the other. The next day she learned that she had lived through the worst earthquake California had ever known. Soon hundreds of homeless and starving people engulfed the town where she lived. The generosity of her mother and others toward these helpless people would be a picture she would carry in her mind forever.

Years later she would say, "Each person was a little child in friendliness and warmth." So how could people continue to be unkind to one another, knowing how much suffering and poverty went on in the world around them?

Devoted to social action, Dorothy Day spent years struggling to make a living writing about things most people did not want to hear. She understood what it was like to be poor, as she had little money for clothes or even adequate housing. She understood how it felt to be imprisoned, because several of the causes she wrote about landed her in jail. She understood how it felt to be hungry, because she had joined hunger strikes protesting unfair treatment of women. And she understood what it was like to be lonely, because she'd been rejected by the people closest to her. The father of her child had left them both when she'd had the baby baptized Catholic. Less than a year later she was baptized herself.

Dorothy decided the best way to combat these many evils was through community. Living in community, one would never be hungry or unnoticed or unloved. But where would such a community come from? As if in answer, she met Peter Maurin, a French immigrant and former religious who embraced a social order founded on gospel values. Together with Maurin, Dorothy Day started a daily newspaper called *The Catholic Worker* and published it for only one cent. It was her way of making sure that everyone could afford it. The first issue was published on May 1, 1933, and contained articles condemning child labor and racial inequality. The paper was an immediate success, soon reaching a daily circulation of 100,000. But *The Catholic Worker* was more than a newspaper; it became the foundation for a lay movement of social justice, a way to live the gospel message of love by serving the poor through voluntary poverty.

Within the year, Dorothy Day opened her home as a shelter to the poor calling it a House of Hospitality. She offered humble meals of soup and bread along with a place to sleep. It was the Depression, and many were without work or food. Soon her house was too small to take in all those who needed her hospitality, and she had to move to a bigger location. Other Houses of Hospitality followed to hold the growing numbers.

During World War II, Dorothy continued to advocate peace. As this was a "popular" war, her position did not win her new friends, and she lost many of the old ones. She declared herself a pacifist, practiced civil disobedience, was jailed again, and in later years spoke out against the horrors of nuclear war. All the while she was labeled an anarchist, communist, and socialist. Throughout the rest of her life, she actively expressed her strong opinions on the suffering of the poor, regardless of what others thought of her. "Everyone is Christ," she said.

For Further Reading

The Long Loneliness by Dorothy Day (San Francisco: Harper San Francisco, 1997).

Dorothy Day: Friend to the Forgotten by Deborah Kent (Grand Rapids: Eerdmans, 1996).

Catherine de Hueck Doherty

Russia, 1896–1985

Wife, mother, writer, social activist

Convert to Catholicism

Founder of Friendship House and Madonna House

"Love-love-love, never counting the cost."

At the age of fifteen, Catherine already showed the headstrong behavior that would later mature into determination. The young Russian girl had fallen in love and, despite her family's wishes, she married the man. He was higher in the aristocracy than her father; when she married, she became a baroness, a title that followed her for the rest of her life.

But after the Russian revolution, life changed suddenly. Family members were killed. Knowing their lives were threatened, both Catherine and her husband became refugees. They nearly died several times crossing Europe, then finally were able to flee to Canada, where a son, George, was born in 1921. After the child's birth, Catherine worked to support her family. They experienced tremendous poverty and hardship, and her marriage did not survive.

It was during this part of her life that Catherine fell in love with God. She had been raised in a devout Russian Orthodox family. Her parents had lived the gospel message of love, and no stranger or beggar was ever turned from their door. Now it was Catherine's turn to live the gospel. Years later she summed up this experience: "And then, one day, the Lord will tap your shoulder and say, 'Now is the time to go on a pilgrimage, into the sea of silence.'" By then she had become a popular lecturer, describing her extraordinary experiences as a refugee. She had grown quite wealthy again, yet the call to pilgrimage seemed to ask her to do something else. In fact, as she put it, she was "mightily bothered" by the Holy Spirit to take action of some kind. And so she did. "Like so many sinners before me, I finally said 'yes' to God."

Catherine's pilgrimage meant seeing God in the poor and in everyone she met. Drawing from her experience, she saw everyone as a refugee who was to be welcomed by God's people on earth. To begin living this new life, she set aside money for her son's care, gave the rest of her considerable new wealth away, then started Friendship House. This was an organization of lay people who served the poor and tried to live according to Franciscan spirituality. Eventually there were houses in several cities in Canada and in Harlem in the United States.

Just because Catherine said yes to God did not mean her vocation would be without trials. Friendship House was a failure. Her motives and methods were questioned, her decision to remarry rather than remain celibate was attacked, and all the houses eventually closed. Packing her things, feeling rejected, she moved back to Canada with her second husband with the idea of leading a quiet life.

That's where she took another plunge into the sea of silence. At this time, her vision sharpened and became clear, embracing again a love for God, people, and the world. "I looked at the Church again," Catherine said. "There she was, beautiful, shining. I realized that she was the Bride of Christ....She passed in front of my eyes, emerging out of the deep silence into which I had been thrust."

Catherine started Madonna House in Combermere, Ontario, Canada. Considering herself a blend of East and West, she steeped Madonna House in Russian spirituality. Soon others came to her and they formed a community that embraced poverty, chastity, and obedience while serving the poor of the area. She also introduced the idea of *poustinia*, Russian for a desert experience of prayer and solitude in which one meets God. The Madonna House community was sanctioned by the church, and they lived under the direction of the bishop of Ontario.

By the time of Catherine's death, there were sixteen Madonna Houses; now there are many more. Her vision of loving and helping people has been embraced by countries all over the world. "If we implement this law of love," she said, "if we clothe it with our flesh, we shall become a light to the world."

Further Reading

Molchanie: The Silence of God by Catherine de Hueck Doherty (New York: Crossroad, 1984).

Fragments of My Life: A Memoir by Catherine de Hueck Doherty (Combermere, Ontario: Madonna House Publications, 1996).

They Called Her the Baroness: The Life of Catherine Doherty by Lorene Hanley Duquin (New York: Alba House, 1995).

$\mathcal{M}$other $\mathcal{K}$atharine $\mathcal{D}$rexel

United States, 1858–1955

Teacher, missionary, and founder of the Sisters of the Blessed Sacrament

Founded dozens of schools and missions for African and Native Americans

Founded Xavier University, the first Catholic college for African Americans

"Love is little things."

Young Kate Drexel sat listening to the priest seated across the dining-room table from her, as he spoke with passion to her cool, logical, investment-banker father. She could hardly believe what Bishop O'Conner was saying. The bishop, a long-time family friend, had recently returned from the "Wild West." Yet instead of exciting stories about cowboys and unknown places, he described all kinds of mistreatment of the American Indian at the hands of the U.S. government.

The bishop spoke of broken treaties and broken promises for food and education. He also described the practice of collecting the Native Americans onto pieces of land called reservations. How could her government not keep its word once it had given it? Kate wondered. Were the Indians really starving? Was there no one to help them?

When her father died, Kate Drexel inherited, along with her sisters, an enormous amount of money. She began to devote herself to the plight of the country's two groups of "outsiders," Native Americans and African Americans. In the second half of the nineteenth century, the Native Americans were a contained problem, left to fend for themselves on reservations without income or resources. They suffered the transition from a life rich in tradition to the "white way" of doing things. Also in this post–Civil War era, African Americans were "freed," yet left on their own. Without education, income, or adequate jobs, they settled into the poorest sections of the country. It was into these areas that Kate Drexel placed her substantial vision and fortune.

In 1889, Katharine received permission to become a religious. Although she wanted to live a cloistered life, she instead founded the Sisters of the Blessed Sacrament, an order expressly devoted to service of the Native American and African American communities. She and her sisters spent their lives building missions and schools and rebuilding schools that had been neglected, threatened, deserted, or even burned out. How should the sisters approach these two groups? "We must attract them by joy," wrote Mother Drexel, "in order to lead them to its source, the Heart of Christ...to Him who is the essential joy of the Father."

No one frightened away Mother Drexel once she decided to open a school. She personally established schools for African Americans in thirteen states and dozens of missions and schools for Native Americans. She also funded the beginning of Xavier

University in New Orleans. This was the first Catholic college for African Americans, which later saw such prestigious graduates as Thea Bowman.

Mother Drexel had a heart attack at the age of seventy-six, which ended her more active work. She spent her remaining twenty years in constant prayer. Her life was one of total self-giving as she helped two peoples create a future for themselves and their children.

For Further Reading

American Women of Faith by Rawley Myers (Huntington, Ind.: Our Sunday Visitor, 1989).

Maria Faustina

Poland, 1905–1938

Member of the Congregation of Sisters of Our Lady of Mercy

Prophet, visionary,
"Apostle of Mercy"

First saint of the new millennium

"May the greatest of all divine attributes, that of...unfathomable mercy, pass through my heart and soul to my neighbor."

As third in a line of ten children, Helena Kowalska found there was always someone to take care of, always something to do. Since she was needed at home, she attended school for only three years. Then, as a teenager, she became a domestic servant to send money home for her family. But this young woman held within her a secret, burning love.

By the time she was almost twenty, she could no longer wait. She decided to devote herself fully to the service of God and joined the Congregation of the Sisters of Our Lady of Mercy in Krakow, Poland. As she died to her old self, a new one was born—Sister Maria Faustina.

Because of her lack of education, Sister Faustina's tasks within the order were considered lowly. She would never be a teacher or spiritual director. She would never be qualified to be head of her order. But ambition was not within her nature. All she wanted to do was help others. She served her order as cook, gardener, and finally doorkeeper, humble roles of relative insignificance.

One day in February, Sister Faustina received a vision that was at once powerful and comforting. It came at a time of great political unrest. Poland's neighbor to the west, Germany, was in turmoil, with the new Nazi Party beginning to gain power. Meanwhile, Poland had its own problems, affected by the worldwide economic slowdown. Thousands began to despair of being able to feed and clothe their families.

But the vision sent to Sister Faustina was one of hope for the individual. In her visions, Jesus asked her to become his secretary and his apostle, as well as a model of mercy to others. His message was that the world would not know peace until it had turned to him in trust and that his mercy was greater than all the world's sins.

Sister Faustina told no one about the visions except a handful of people. After passing a psychiatric exam, she was ordered by her confessor to record her visions, as many of the church's greatest contemplatives had done before her. The result was a journal hundreds of pages long. This was remarkable in itself, since she could neither read nor write well because of her poor education.

For four years she wrote, all the while continuing in her humble duties. Many sisters of her order knew nothing. Yet soon after her early death at the age of thirty-three, word spread about these visions that cried out the message of God's divine mercy. Her work was at first suppressed, because it had been mistranslated from the Polish. Ultimately it was accepted, and her cause for sainthood was put forth by a young priest who had read her diaries in the original. The young priest later became Pope John Paul II.

Today Mercy Sunday is celebrated as a feast day around the world, a day of extraordinary hope given us by this simple, uneducated Polish woman.

For Further Reading

The Diary of Saint Maria Faustina: Divine Mercy in My Soul by Faustina Kowalska (Stockbridge, Mass.: Marian Press, 2000).

The Life of Faustina Kowalska: The Authorized Biography by Sophia Michalenko (Ann Arbor: Charis Books, 1999).

Maria Goretti

Italy, 1890–1902

Murdered defending her virginity

Forgave her murderer
on her deathbed

Youngest saint in the
Catholic Church

"For the love of Jesus, I forgive him...."

Eleven-year-old Maria looked forward to her First Communion. It was to be a special day set aside for bringing her closer to God. Since the death of her father from malaria three years earlier, days of such joy were few. Maria had had to take over the monotonous household duties while her mother ran the farm. But the girl performed her tasks obediently and cheerfully. Her devotion to the Blessed Mother encouraged her in her work.

The daughter of poverty, Maria Goretti lived in a small town in Italy, where her family shared a large building with another family. For three years after her father died, her life revolved around everyday domestic chores, as well as the heavy labor that would have been reserved for him. Despite the hardships of such a life, she was beautiful and mature for her age, and attracted the interest of a young man almost ten years older than she was. Without the protection of a father, she was stalked and threatened by the man. She resisted his sexual advances, insisting that they were wrong. Furious, he ended up stabbing her fourteen times. She did not die until the next day. Before her death, she forgave the young man and prayed for him.

Jailed for the murder, the man remained violent for years until Maria appeared to him in a vision. He immediately reformed his life, and when his sentence was finally served, he became a Capuchin brother. He lived to see his victim canonized as a saint.

Maria Goretti is a saint for individuals trying to keep their purity despite outside pressure. She also represents the struggle of all women who suffer at the hands of overwhelming power. She's a symbol of the body's sacredness, a resounding *No!* to the violations inflicted by war, political oppression, individual violence, or family abuse. At the same time, her death is a lesson in forgiveness, a lesson in breaking the cycle of violence through love, even love for her own murderer.

For Further Reading

A Year with the Saints: Quotations and Extracts for Every Day of the Year by Mark Water (Liguori, Mo: Liguori Publications, 1997).

The Book of Christian Martyrs by Bruno Chenu et al (New York: Crossroad, 1990).

José Hobday

United States, 1929–

*Native American,
of Seneca Iroquois
and half-Seminole parents*

Sister of St. Francis of Assisi

Writer, professor, international speaker

Itinerant preacher among Native Americans
and the marginalized

"Wherever Jesus went, he created abundance."

As José did her homework in the family living room, she could hear the voices of her parents from the kitchen. One evening they were discussing how to ration the meager funds they had to cover bills and expenses for the following week. José began to worry. It was obvious to her that they would not have enough left for food. How would they survive?

Suddenly her mother walked in, gave her some mney, and told her to take her brothers with her to get strawberry ice cream. José wasn't sure this was the right thing to do in view of the conversation she'd just overheard. She went into the other room and asked her father if the money should really be spent on ice cream. He told her it should.

Once José returned home with the big bags of ice cream, her mother turned on music and opened the doors to the house. She went out and invited all the neighbors to an ice cream treat. As José later saw it, her parents were teaching them that they needed to abandon themselves to the grace and kindness of God. God's family never goes hungry.

José Hobday is the daughter of a Seneca Iroquois mother and a half-Seminole father who was a Baptist. Her father converted to Catholicism in his teens. When her mother accepted his offer of marriage, she was quickly disowned by the Lutheran family who had adopted her, but she married anyway. Her mother never looked back and she, too, converted to Catholicism.

Both of her parents became powerful spiritual influences on José. Her father always loved the Catholic Church because "he saw more riffraff there than in any other church." Her mother loved the church's rituals that blended well with her own Native American traditions. José felt extremely blessed all her young life.

After becoming a Franciscan sister, José became an educator and taught school on several reservations in the Southwest. Naturally drawn to a contemplative way of thinking, she found simplicity to be the key to happiness. "You can expect from simplicity a freedom of spirit you can hardly believe," she asserts. "Simplicity erodes stress."

Today Sister José serves the poor, street youth, and imprisoned women. She also teaches college. And she's an itinerant preacher, crossing the nation to give lectures, retreats, and discussions on such varied issues as living simply, Native American spirituality, women in the church, and peace and justice. She has made great inroads in combining her native traditions with Christian ones. Some of these ideas are making prayer creation centered, gaining a love and respect for silence, living in harmony with nature, and keeping alive the memory of others through story telling.

Sister José Hobday celebrates life in its creation. With an infectious sense of humor, she easily dispels any worries about the world. She is an ambassador for hope in the future. As her mother once told her, "Until you can put your arms around all of life, which includes death and dying, you will never really understand life."

For Further Reading

Stories of Awe and Abundance by Sister José Hobday, O.S.F. (Franklin, Wis.: Sheed & Ward, 1995).

You Chose Well (audiotape) by Sister José Hobday, O.S.F. (Kansas City, Mo.: Credence Cassettes, 1994).

Voices of the Winds: Native American Legends by Margot Edmonds and Ella E. Clark (New York: Facts on File, 1989).

Juana Inés de la Cruz

Mexico, 1651–1695

Poet, playwright, and prose writer

Sister of the Order of St. Jerome

First great poet of the New World

First feminist of the New World

"When love is placed in God, nothing else can intervene."

From the moment of her birth, everything in her life would embrace the unbelievable. Juana de Asbajey Ramirez was born in 1651 to unmarried parents in a small village south of Mexico City. Able to read by the age of three, Juana developed such a thirst for knowledge that it's said she pleaded with her mother to allow her to dress as a boy in order to attend classes at the university nearby. She was seven.

Juana then went to live with her grandfather. He had an immense library, which she quickly exhausted. It was plain that she meant to embrace every piece of knowledge of the world that she could find, never thinking that her position as a woman should discourage her interest. She taught herself Latin, literature, philosophy, science, and mathematics. Presented at court at thirteen, she became well known for her writing and for her engaging debates with the male intellects of the day. She was labeled a child prodigy. Widely known for her beauty, she turned down many offers of marriage. It's debated today whether she refused from devotion to the church, unwillingness to be ruled by a husband, or disillusionment with love ("You've made me lose all,/ yet no, losing all/ is not paying too dear/ for being undeceived").

Taking the name Juana Inés de la Cruz, she entered the convent, first joining the Discalced Carmelites of St. Joseph in Mexico City, then the much more liberal Convent of the Order of Saint Jerome. There she was able to keep up with her intellectual pursuits, studying theology, medicine, canon law, astronomy, and advanced mathematics. She continued to write, finishing plays, poems, and many prose pieces that she was commissioned to do at court, as well as sacred works. She also taught drama and music to girls.

Juana felt that women had biblical and theological rights to educational opportunities that corresponded to their interests and gifts and that they should not be limited to embroidery and household duties. As her fame became international, her intellectual habits and writings came under scrutiny. In 1694, the church hierarchy felt that she was overstepping herself and her religious life. She was ordered to dispose of her scientific equipment, musical instruments, and her library of four thousand books, the largest in the New World. She was also told to stop writing because she wrote so much secular literature. She did as she was told and signed a document expressing her humility and obedience to church authority.

Within a year plague and famine struck Mexico and Sor Juana died tending to the sick in her convent.

Today, Juana Inés de la Cruz has been rediscovered and is hailed as the first Hispanic feminist, a defender of educational options for women, and the greatest poet the American continent was to produce in the seventeenth century.

For Further Reading

Wise Women: Over 2000 Years of Spiritual Writing by Women edited by Susan Cahill (New York: W.W. Norton, 1996).

Chiara Lubich

Italy, 1920–

Founder of the Focalare movement

Worker for Christian unity and interreligious dialogue

Writer and international speaker

"If we love one another, then the world will believe."

Chiara Lubich, a young Italian teacher, tried to keep her elementary school students focused on their studies. But their gazes strayed out the windows of the country schoolhouse. How could anyone focus on learning as war raged around them? Nearby was the once bustling city of Trent, a beautiful blend of past and present. Bombs dropped daily on the historic city, and the dead were counted among every family.

Chiara could not rationalize war on any level. She watched the deprivations placed on the elderly. She watched impetuous and joyful youth cut down like hay as war reaped its harvest. She heard the cries of women giving birth, knowing both mother and child would be devoured by the open jaws of the Nazi war machine. The world was falling apart around her. What consolation was left?

In 1943, against the backdrop of World War II, twenty-three-year-old Chiara Lubich and her friends opened their Bibles seeking answers to the horrific devastation around them. The words of sacred scripture seemed to sparkle with truth and ignited a flame in their minds and hearts. "These words [of Jesus] appeared to us as spellbinding: they possessed tremendous majesty; they were words of life to be translated into life." Chiara felt the Word of God move so deeply within her that it could not be ignored.

She and her friends began meeting on a regular basis in an air raid shelter. As the bombs exploded outside, they would study a scripture quote, one phrase at a time. Through the sharing of their insights, they decided to find ways to apply the quote to their daily lives. They knew this would be difficult to do in the world around them so they created a community to encourage one another. The selected scripture verses that they collected and studied were soon called the "Word of Life," because they were meant to be applied throughout the day to ordinary situations as they occurred. Chiara felt that scripture was to be lived once the Bible was closed, not just meditated upon.

Soon others began to join Chiara and her friends as they gathered to share their reflections on scripture. The group came to be known as the *focolare*, which is Italian for "hearth." Undeterred by the war, the group dedicated itself to creating peace and unity within the world through the gospel message of love.

World War II ended but the little group continued. Much love would be needed to piece together a world torn apart. The

Focolare movement blossomed as more people committed to unity, peace, and justice. Chiara's dream of unity was founded on living out in the world the ideas presented within the gospel message of love.

In 1958 other religions started to take note of Chiara Lubich's movement. Several Protestant organizations thought it might be worthwhile and visited the Focolare in Italy to understand their way of life. They were so impressed by what they saw that they joined the movement themselves, still committed to Protestant practices and beliefs, but now more aware of living the gospel and of its possibilities for action in the world.

In 1981, Chiara was invited to speak in front of ten thousand Buddhists in Japan. There she shared her ideas of the Christian experience and unity. This proved instrumental in promoting better understanding between two major world belief systems. Focolare is now a member of the World Conference on Religion and Peace.

Out of war came Chiara's single idea, that love can conquer all. There are new "Hitlers" today, new divisions among people, and new hatreds, but the gospel message of love is still being lived, acted on, and transformed into a source of hope by the people of the Focalare. The movement now has over eighty-seven thousand formal members and two million supporters in almost two hundred countries, embracing people of all ages, all nations, and all religions and beliefs.

For Further Reading

A Call to Love by Chiara Lubich (Hyde Park, N.Y.: New City Press, 1989).

Chiara Lubich

From Scripture to Life by Chiara Lubich (Hyde Park, N.Y.: New City Press, 1991).

Chiara Lubich: A Life of Unity by Franca Zanbonini (Hyde Park, N.Y.: New City Press, 1992).

Mother Mary MacKillop

Australian, 1842–1909

Writer, teacher, and founder of the Sisters of St. Joseph of the Sacred Heart

Provided education, health care, and hope for the poor of Australia

Founded over forty schools

Once excommunicated, is now a saint

"Bear with one another as God bears with each of us."

The teacher stood at the front of the class explaining the history of Mary Queen of Scots. Even though nineteenth-century students were expected to listen in silence, ten-year-old Mary MacKillop raised her voice in protest. The bright daughter of a Scottish immigrant to Australia, she told the teacher that the depiction of the queen given in the textbook was untrue. Mary was promptly told to be quiet, a message she would hear throughout her life. Her outspokenness was a virtue, yet one that would torment her. At the same time, she eventually learned that silence and patience yielded their own rewards.

Knowing how difficult it was for any Australian child to get a good education, the adult Mary made teaching the backbone of her life's work. In 1867, with the help of a local priest, she founded a group of women religious devoted to teaching the poorest of the poor. Their institute was called the Sisters of St. Joseph of the Sacred Heart, or Josephites, and they embraced a philosophy of following the quiet, humble way of St. Joseph. Their rule encompassed several ideals: to live a life of poverty, to depend only on Divine Providence, to allow each community of sisters to be governed from within, and to go wherever they were needed.

Going where they were needed meant the sisters followed farmers into the harsh Australian outback. The sisters packed wagons and hauled books, following railway workers whose lives were scattered along rows of tiny towns. And the sisters traveled to mining communities as bleak and barren as the scorched earth the miners worked. In each place the Josephites gave the children both a free education and a future of hope. The sisters also provided homes for the elderly and terminally ill, help for neglected children and their families, and orphanages for the many homeless children scattered across the continent.

As difficult as all these challenges were, God had other tests for Mary, or "presents" as she called them. The bishops of Australia rejected the Rule she had written for her community. They did not want the sisters to be self-governed, but wished each community to be under the local bishop. They also wanted to be rid of Mary, the Josephites' troublemaking mother general. They were so intent on bending her will to theirs that they interfered with her work, spread lies about her, and finally excommunicated her. Bishop Sheil, who pronounced the judgment upon her, accused her of having "incited the sisters to disobedience and defiance."

Mary refused to break the Rule of her own order, which would have allowed the bishops to dispose of the sisters however they pleased. Her Rule and her order relied on direction from Rome only. And so Mary went to the pope himself for authorization. Despite his approval, despite her reinstatement, and despite a deathbed confession of wrongdoing from Bishop Sheil, on her return she was again subjected to public slander and embarrassment by the bishops. They told her that a "commission" had arrived from Rome to investigate the nuns personally. This "commission" led to extensive hours of grueling interrogation. The sisters' lives were in constant upheaval, their records were searched, and their private diaries were read. The commission sought out anyone who could provide evidence against the mother general. The process went on for months before the truth was revealed: Rome had authorized no such investigation. Once again, it was the local bishops not wanting the Josephites to be governed from within. In the midst of it all, Mary patiently complied with the commission's demands and encouraged her sisters to cooperate however they could.

In spite of the bad publicity, school attendance soared, a tribute to the Josephites. Many people recognized that the sisters were being persecuted and became staunch friends and contributors. Surprisingly, the largest groups of supporters were Protestants and Jews. They saw the many benefits to society of the sisters' hard work and so provided for them.

When Mary MacKillop died in 1909, she left an order with over one hundred sisters, a Rule approved by the Holy See, and over forty schools in Adelaide, Queensland, New

South Wales, and New Zealand. During her last years she bore great physical suffering, but those tending to her remarked on her strength and inner calm, all grounded in a union with Jesus Christ and his crucifixion. She proved capable of "running the good race," as St. Paul said—and of winning.

For Further Reading

An Extraordinary Australian: Mary MacKillop by Paul Gardiner, S.J. (Newton, Australia: E. J. Dwyer and David Ell Press, 1994).

Mary MacKillop Unveiled by Lesley O'Brien (Victoria, Australia: CollinsDove, 1994).

Raïssa Maritain

Russia, 1883–1960

*Wife, poet, mystic,
contemplative*

Convert to Catholicism

Partner and inspiration to the
one of the greatest theologians
of the 20th century

"To know what is...."

Young Raïssa was confused and bewildered by what was expected in her new school. Her Jewish family had just fled across Europe from Russia, and she, her sister Vera, and their mother and father were trying very hard to settle into the busy world of France as soon as possible. The language was different, but Raïssa would try her best to be the model student she had been in Russia. It took her only two weeks.

Raïssa Oumansov fell in love with France and everything about it, especially the language. There was something in its beauty that connected her to feelings she could not describe. At just sixteen, she went to the Sorbonne where she studied science. She wanted to know the truth of life, "to know what is...," and at this point she felt science was the field that would best help her. Yet scientific rationalism gave her no more satisfaction than the materialism that had spread throughout nineteenth-century France.

When Raïssa met the man who would change her life forever, the two were both college students looking for answers to the same questions, especially about God and human suffering. Jacques Maritain was passing around a petition, zealously attempting to get signatures to support a social cause. Raïssa signed the paper. Their lives became immediately entwined. But even while they shared great love for each other, they also shared a painful desperation about the meaningless of existence. "We swam aimlessly in the waters of observation and experience like a fish in the depths of the sea, without ever seeing the sun whose dim rays filtered down to us....And sadness pierced me, the bitter taste of the emptiness of a soul which saw the lights go out, one by one."

Raïssa and Jacques Maritain married on November 26, 1904. Despite their despair, something in them would not allow them to give up. Their continued search for meaning ultimately led them to certain Catholic philosophers and writers. Within two years of their marriage, the Maritains both converted. Catholicism helped Raïssa make sense of the world's suffering, especially, as the decades passed, the suffering inflicted by Germany. Raïssa saw in the ordeal of the Jews an arrow pointing to Christ, a fellow Jew; she saw in their ordeal a sign that Christians should unite their own sufferings with his. Yet this wasn't just an intellectual exercise. Reacting to the horrors of World War II from the safety of her own life, Raïssa wrote, "Don't imagine that faith and hope bring spiritual comfort. It is true that they ward off despair, but the burden of such comfort would destroy them."

Well known in France and later in America, Jacques Maritain lived a vital, active life. Their home was a magnet for artists and intellectuals. Within this whirl of activity, Raïssa became a contemplative, cloistered within her home, devoting long hours to prayer, meditation, and her journal. She was also gifted in poetry, and often it was only through poetry that she could express the yearning for God she felt so acutely.

Raïssa's quiet life stood in contrast to that of her husband, who became one of the twentieth century's greatest Catholic theologians. Jacques never failed to give her equal credit when speaking of his own success. Her life inspired him. Yet even he did not realize the full depth of her soul until after her death when he read her journals. Raïssa Maritain is now considered one of the greatest contemplatives of modern times.

Throughout her life Raïssa traveled from despair to belief, from confusion to calm, from the uncertainty of whether God acted in the world to the certainty that he was always present. "And everything that can be saved will be saved."

Further Reading

Raïssa Maritain: Raïssa's Journal, presented by Jacques Maritain (Albany: Magi Books, 1974).

Raïssa Maritain: Pilgrim, Poet, Exile by Judith D. Suther (New York: Fordham University Press, 1990).

Zelie Martin

France, 1831–1877

Wife, business owner, and mother of nine, five of whom entered religious life

Mother of Thérèse of Lisieux, doctor of the church

"I love children to the point of folly."

Zelie Guerin spent her childhood feeling unloved and misunderstood. Her father was a soldier before settling down as a constable in the French town of Gandelain, now known as Orne. There he married a peasant woman. Of the three children born to them, the son was clearly favored, and an older sister later went into the convent. Zelie felt called to the cloistered religious life as well, but she was deemed not worthy of the vocation by a local priest.

Deciding to make her way in the business world, she learned to make Alençon lace, which was highly prized, and in 1853, at the age of twenty-two, opened her own business. Five years later she met Louis Martin, a watchmaker, who had also dreamed of entering the religious life and had also been rejected. He offered her a marriage where they would live together in celibacy, as brother and sister, and she agreed.

Their confessor persuaded them to drop such restrictions on their marriage, and within ten years they had nine children.

"I love children to the point of folly," Zelie said. "I was born to have them...." She showered on them all the love she herself had been denied as a girl. Deeply devout, she prayed that one of her children would be a priest, a missionary, or a saint. Yet three died in early infancy and one at the age of five. Their deaths were a terrible test of a mother's faith, but Zelie held on firmly, especially to her devotion to Mary. Mary understood a mother's tears.

When Zelie found herself pregnant for what would be the final time, she also found a lump in her breast. "If God gives me the grace to nurse this child, it would only be a pleasure to rear it." Soon she became the mother of a fifth daughter. She named the beautiful little girl Thérèse.

When the infant became weak, Zelie sent her to the country to live for the first year with a wet nurse. It was a difficult separation, but Zelie was determined to save her daughter if she could. When Thérèse was finally brought home, no child could have been more pampered. Zelie continued to work at her lace business, now with her husband involved in the day-to-day operations as well, but she never forgot to fill her house with the two things most important to her, faith and love. Daily Mass, prayer, and family devotions were the heart of all other activities.

Zelie died from breast cancer when Thérèse was only four and a half, but her influence had already directed her youngest onto the path to sainthood.

All five of Zelie Martin's daughters entered the cloistered life, and her youngest was declared a saint less than thirty years after her death. Thérèse was also declared a doctor of the church in 1997, only the third woman to receive such a title. Zelie's part in creating the atmosphere of faith that led to this extraordinary family is just one reason why she herself, together with her husband, is now in the process of canonization.

Further Reading

Zelie Martin: Mother of St. Thérèse of Lisieux by Louis and Marjorie Wust (Boston: St. Paul Editions, 1959 and 1969).

The Story of a Life: St. Thérèse of Lisieux by Guy Gaucher (New York: Harper and Row, 1987).

Autobiography of St. Thérèse of Lisieux, translated by Ronald Knox (New York: P. J. Kenedy and Sons 1957).

Mary of the Incarnation

France, 1566–1618

Wife, mother, and religious
supporter

Defended her husband's honor
in court

Brought the Ursulines and the
Carmelites to France

Entered the Carmelite order before her death

"The beauty of a virtuous wife is
the radiance of her home."

Barbara Avrillot at first wanted to be a nun. She had made a pilgrimage with her mother to Liesse in 1572. Also, she had spent many years as an intern student at the order house of St. Clare near Paris. So it was natural that Barbara felt a strong pull to the religious life. But she was the only child to have survived infancy out of six children. Her parents did not want her to enter the convent. They wanted her to marry and bear heirs, for everyone's future.

So in 1584, Barbara Avrillot married Pierre Acarie, a wealthy young man who enjoyed a high position of authority among the French nobility. But this was during the Protestant Reformation, and relations between Catholics and Protestants were tense and bitter. Pierre Acarie aligned himself against the succession of a new Protestant king. When Henry IV triumphed and took the throne, Acarie found himself accused of treason. His fortune was seized, and he was exiled. Barbara was left behind in Paris, impoverished and with six children, to deal with creditors.

Barbara wrote letters of petition on her husband's behalf and even appeared in court to defend his honor. She finally had his innocence proclaimed, won his return to Paris, and was granted the return of some of his wealth. Throughout these dark times, her faith grew with the help of spiritual counselors such as Francis de Sales and Vincent de Paul. She also engaged in many charitable works despite her own family's needs, and worked among the poor and the sick.

Convents were usually the only source of education for girls from poor families. Barbara wanted to insure that girls who did not have a religious vocation could also receive a good education, so she helped the Ursulines, a teaching order, expand their role in France. Later she became very interested in the writings of Teresa of Avila and felt strongly that the order of Discalced Carmelites should also be brought to her country. She eventually founded five Carmelite convents. In later years, these would produce the great religious minds of Elizabeth of the Trinity and Thérèse of Lisieux. Barbara's charitable works had the support of many, including the Protestant king.

After her husband's death, Barbara Avrillot became a lay sister, Mary of the Incarnation. She retired to the Carmelite convent that housed one of her daughters, who later became its assistant superior. On her deathbed Barbara spoke her wishes for the sisters gathered around her: "If it should please Almighty God to admit me to eternal bliss, I will ask that the will of His divine Son should be accomplished in each one of you."

For Further Reading

The Spiritual Teaching of Mary of the Incarnation by Fernand Jette, O.M.I. (Franklin, Wis.: Sheed & Ward, 1963).

Flannery O'Connor

United States, 1925–1964

Fiction writer

Recipient of the
National Book Award

Died of lupus

*"We live in an unbelieving age but one which is
markedly and lopsidedly spiritual."*

As young Flannery sat typing out her manuscript, she
noticed her arms began to feel heavy. The tiredness she had been
experiencing of late could no longer be ignored. She had a feeling she knew what the doctor would tell her. She had seen these
symptoms before—in her father when he had been diagnosed
with the incurable disease that eventually killed him. That disease was lupus erythematosus, a condition in which a person's
immune system attacks rather than protects their body.

By the time Flannery O'Connor was diagnosed with
lupus, she had already received considerable recognition for a
collection of short stories and a novel. But once the strain of
the disease took control of her work day, she decided to return

to her home in Milledgeville, Georgia. There she completed her greatest works in the short time she had left.

O'Connor's subjects were not the usual ones for a young Southern lady writing in the 1950s. "The serious writer has always taken the flaw in human nature as his starting point, usually the flaw in an otherwise admirable character," she said. O'Connor's characters were flawed to the point of grotesqueness, and they often faced violent deaths. There was both dark humor in her writing as well as an unmistakable religious sensibility, in that these grotesque characters were allowed a moment of grace, which they many times refused. The combination was powerful but unsettling, and her stories shocked and disturbed her readers.

That grace existed was more important to her than whether her characters accepted it or not. She explained this, saying that she needed to exaggerate for readers, that for those who saw no evidence at all of grace in the world, "you have to make your vision apparent by shock—to the hard-of-hearing you shout, and for the almost-blind you draw large and startling figures."

Widely proclaimed as one of the greatest Southern and greatest American writers, Flannery O'Connor used her Catholic faith as the foundation for her life and writing, even though her characters and situations were not Catholic. The overall lasting impression of her work is not one of any denomination but of a real and ever-present spiritual mystery in the midst of life.

For Further Reading

Mystery and Manners: Occasional Prose by Flannery O'Connor, selected and edited by Sally and Robert Fitzgerald (New York: Noonday Press, Farrar, Straus & Giroux, 1957).

Flannery O'Connor: The Collected Works by Flannery O'Connor, edited by Sally Fitzgerald (New York: Library of America, 1988).

Maura O'Halloran

United States, 1955–1982

Student of Zen Buddhism

First Westerner and woman
admitted to Japan's
Kannonji Temple

Received Enlightenment in 1982

Catholic-raised Buddhist saint

*"All the time my pulse beats, 'nothingness,
nothingness.' Poems have come to me
between the beats of* mu.*"* *

As the oldest child in her family, Maura O'Halloran learned early the lesson that few things have permanence. She was born in the United States, but her father moved the family to his native Ireland when she was just four. They returned to America when she was eleven. Three years later her father died in an accident. The remaining O'Hallorans moved back to Ireland, where Maura matured quickly and became a second parent to her five siblings.

Mu was given to O'Halloran for meditation. It means nothingness or absence, a state of being without; it has also been interpreted as a nonsense word.

Maura was accepted into Trinity College in Dublin and later received their highest scholastic award. During the summers she worked with drug addicts and the poor of Dublin and at a school for children with autism and disabilities in Northern Ireland. She also traveled to Italy, Greece, North Africa, France, the United Kingdom, and—after graduation— Canada and Latin America. In these places she moved among the poor and lived a very simple life, always aware of others' poverty and suffering.

O'Halloran was on a quest, searching the world for an answer to an unknown question. All she had was a beginning interest in meditation. The rest she trusted would find its way to her. Finally, in 1979, her quest brought her to a small and out-of-the-way Buddhist temple in Japan.

In her journal, Maura writes, "There are four monks like little boys, laughing, innocent, delighted to see me. I meet the master, Go Roshi. When I was told that I could stay there, I felt as if I had come home, very settled and bursting with happiness." In the discipline of Zen Buddhism Maura at last found the answer to her quest.

What is Zen? A Cistercian monk of this century, Thomas Merton, said that Zen could not be analyzed logically. It is "not a religion, not a philosophy, not a system of thought, not a doctrine...."—yet on the surface it may appear to be all those things. Because of this, it is difficult for Westerners to understand. At that time, in the late 1970s, very few Western men had attempted training in Zen Buddhism, and even fewer women. Maura was a pioneer on this path to meaning.

After arriving at the temple, she devoted the next three years of her life to understanding Zen. Her accomplishments and self discipline astounded the monks. She completed one thousand days of continuous Zen practice, a feat unheard of for a Western woman. As a Buddhist nun, she worked long hours cooking, cleaning, tending the garden, all considered favored duties. These trusted assignments were given only to those thought capable of sustaining the lives of the monks at the temple. In 1982, after one thousand days and countless hours of meditation, rituals, and sleepless nights, she reached her Enlightenment, an emptying of herself to reach a full understanding of life.

Once she reached "Enlightenment," she headed for home. She decided to delay her journey back to the United States by taking a trip through Thailand. There she was killed in a bus accident during a tour. She was just twenty-seven years old.

"I feel ecstatically happy," she had written in her journal during the last year of her life. "It's a gorgeous May, warm and breezy. I love the world."

Maura O'Halloran—Irish-American Catholic-born Buddhist nun—had come into a consciousness that few find, an awareness of the poor and suffering, an appreciation for the little things so often taken for granted. A statue dedicated to her stands today in the same temple where she received Enlightenment. It gives O'Halloran the name "Great Enlightened Lady, of the same heart and mind as the Great Teacher Buddha."

Further Reading

Pure Heart, Enlightened Mind: The Zen Journal and Letters of Maura "Soshin" O'Halloran by Maura O'Halloran, introduction by Ruth O'Halloran (Boston: Charles E. Tuttle, 1994).

Rosa Parks

United States, 1913–

Wife, speaker, writer, and activist for African Americans

Triggered the Civil Rights movement

Awarded Presidential Medal of Freedom

"You must know who you are, where you are, and where you have been so that you will know where you are going."

Eleven-year-old Rosa was eager to start school. After being taught at home, she was finally being enrolled at the Montgomery Industrial School for Girls, known for encouraging self-esteem in young women. Her mother always told her to "take advantage of the opportunities, no matter how few they are." What she meant was, no matter how few they were for African Americans.

Alabama and other Southern states had segregation laws that separated African Americans from whites. They not only lived, worked, and were educated separately in situations of inferior quality, but were also kept apart in public places. African Americans had separate entrances to buildings, separate water fountains, separate restrooms, and so on. While they were allowed to ride the same buses as whites, they had to pay their fare to the driver, get out of the bus and re-enter by a rear door, then sit or stand in the back of the bus, even if seats were available up front. Also, while the country's Constitution gave them the right to vote, laws in individual states made it impossible to do so.

This was the world in which Rosa grew up. Her mother's advice to "take advantage of opportunities, no matter how few they are" inspired Rosa to finish her high school education. Because of her own and her mother's poor health, that didn't happen until 1934, two years after Rosa was married to Raymond Parks in Pine Level, Alabama.

The young couple joined a local chapter of the NAACP, or National Association for the Advancement of Colored People. Being "second-class citizens" had become intolerable for them. They felt strongly that the time had come for action to be taken on behalf of all people of color.

Rosa attempted to register to vote but was turned away. She was forced off buses by the drivers because she refused to re-enter through the back door after having paid her fare. As years went by, she became increasingly more angry. Besides the complex segregation rules, African Americans also faced the physical danger of jail, beatings, and even murder.

Her frustration bubbled over one night as she boarded the bus to go home after an exhausting day at work. She was asked to give up her seat so a white man could sit down. She refused. Her decision was spontaneous, yet was supported by her years of working toward justice. "I have learned over the years that when one's mind is made up, this diminishes fear."

When Rosa refused to move, the police were called. She was taken to jail, fingerprinted, and left to sit in a cell alone. Later that evening, she was released when friends found out where she was and posted bail.

In the following days she became a symbol that inspired the largest movement for rights within the twentieth century— the Civil Rights movement. It began with a massive bus strike by African Americans and ultimately led to the end of segregation. Because of Rosa Parks's actions, boycotts, protests, and sit-ins became household words, and two landmark rulings were handed down by the Supreme Court: the Civil Rights Act of 1964 and the Voting Rights Act of 1965.

Though she was personally harassed in the following months and years, Rosa Parks continued to fight for justice. She joined the staff of a U.S. representative. She lectured extensively on civil rights and received many awards and honorary degrees from around the world. She also cofounded the Rosa and Raymond Parks Institute for Self-Development to help young people achieve their potential.

For Further Reading

Rosa Parks: My Story by Rosa Parks, with James Haskins (New York: Dial Books, 1992).

Quiet Strength by Rosa Parks, with Gregory J. Reed (Grand Rapids: Zondervan, 2000).

Helen Prejean

United States, 1938–

Teacher, writer, Sister of St. Joseph of Medaille

Activist against the death penalty

Wrote *Dead Man Walking*, nominated for the Pulitzer Prize

Nominated for the Nobel Peace Prize several times

"Are we here to persecute our brothers or bring compassion into a world which is cruel without reason?"

Helen led the privileged life of a wealthy young woman growing up in a Southern town. Her large, loving, professional family guaranteed her a stable future, without worry or too much sacrifice. Helen saw the security given to her within her family and wanted to extend that love to others.

She chose to enter the Sisters of St. Joseph of Medaille, originally founded in France as a way to serve the underprivileged. In the United States, it was an order dedicated to working with the poor of Louisiana. After completing her college work, Helen at first taught junior and senior high school students. Then she took a different path that involved her more immediately in the lives of the poor and society's outsiders.

In 1981 she moved into a housing project for the poor in New Orleans. While there, she was invited to become a pen pal with a convicted killer on death row. Despite having no experience with prisoners, she accepted and wrote letters to cheer him as best she could. She had no idea what crime had been committed, who had been involved, or what the man she wrote to looked like.

Eventually Patrick Sonnier asked her to visit him in the prison. While she was there, he told her he was innocent of the murder he was accused of and asked for her help in an appeal, which she gave. When all appeals had been exhausted and the date set for his execution, Sonnier then asked Sister Helen to be his spiritual advisor. Again, she said yes and helped him prepare for his death in the electric chair. She supported him and was present at the end, even though he ultimately confessed his guilt to her. And at the moment of Patrick Sonnier's execution, something in her was born: a deep conviction of the wrongness of the death penalty.

At the urging of friends, Sister Helen wrote her experiences down, and the book became a best-seller. Through her eyes, others became more aware of the horrors of capital punishment. Yet Sister Helen also helps the victims of crime as well, and started a victim advocacy group in New Orleans. She counsels both prison inmates and their families, as well as the victims' families. She has been sought out by the government for her opinions on the death penalty and has been asked by other countries throughout the world to speak to them on justice, human rights, and the death penalty.

For Further Reading

Dead Man Walking: An Eyewitness Account of the Death Penalty in the United States by Helen Prejean (New York: Vintage Books, 1996).

Welcome to Hell: Letters and Writings from Death Row by Jan Arriens, edited by Helen Prejean (Boston: Northeastern University Press, 1997).

Mollie Rogers

United States, 1882–1955

Founder of the Maryknoll Sisters, the first group of missionary sisters

"There is nothing more astonishing than life, just as it is...."

Little Mollie Rogers knew what it was to be one in a crowd. All seven of her siblings, along with several cousins, stood in line on the sandy beach waiting to be counted by her father. She watched him, his long frame towering over all, counting each head with a precision only King Midas would have had counting his gold. Once the children were all accounted for to his satisfaction, they could scurry back out to swim the cold Atlantic waters, knowing that he would call them in again every so often to count each sacred head.

The idea of being one of many, and extending that idea to everyone in the world, was planted early in Mollie's life. She heard stories from her parents of children in faraway lands, and her own extensive collection of exotic dolls showed just how different others could be. But it did not frighten her. All peoples were reflections of the loving face of God.

It was during Mollie's school years at Roxbury High in Roxbury, Massachusetts, that her leadership skills blossomed. Graduating with honors, she delivered the commencement address to classmates and parents on the topic of "toleration."

After high school she attended Smith College in Northampton, Massachusetts. There were few Catholics attending Smith. One day the Protestant students were rejoicing over missionary activity they had pledged to undertake. Mollie wondered why there was no similar program for Catholic students and decided to form one.

"I was a Catholic and I had known from childhood that there were foreign mission societies which needed help; I had even had idle visions of working for the salvation of souls. The fact was that I had done nothing....From that moment I had work to do, little or great, God alone knew."

With a degree in zoology, Mollie taught school for several years before being hired to do secretarial work for a newly launched magazine entitled *The Field Afar*. Today it is known as *Maryknoll*. *The Field Afar* was the magazine of the Catholic Foreign Mission Society of America, founded by two priests from New York City. The organization sought to train young men for missionary work at a time when the United States was still considered in need of missionaries itself. There were millions of new immigrants seeking to blend in with American society, and many European orders sent religious here to help them.

The organization started by Father Walsh and Father Price was formed to send missionaries outside of the United States. All of these missionaries were men. Mollie believed that women should be sent as well. However, Rome thought that women, especially American women, were too pampered and weak to endure the hardships of such work. Mollie went ahead and found like-minded women willing to try. But Rome would not recognize her group as a community of religious sisters, only as a "Pious Society of Women for Foreign Missions."

Mollie was disappointed but worked harder at spiritual training for the group, getting the help of other religious orders to achieve the same status. In 1920 her group was recognized as the Maryknoll Sisters of St. Dominic. A year later six sisters left the United States to set off for China, and the Maryknoll tradition began. Mollie herself never became a foreign missionary and headed her congregation from this country. But by the time of her death, she had sent over eleven hundred sisters throughout the world.

Mollie Rogers' spiritual ideas and prayer life show her open and honest simplicity. She identified and reflected Christ to the world, and she had a bountiful compassion for her fellow humans. She also felt deeply that she was not separate from anyone. God's presence was in everyone, and through God we were all connected.

"I think it is the cause of the joy that dominates the life of every Maryknoll sister—union with God. We can't talk about it. It's a thing that is too deep; too real; it touches the hidden wells of our hearts...."

For Further Reading

Hearts on Fire: The Story of the Maryknoll Sisters by Penny Lernoux (Maryknoll, N.Y.: Orbis Books, 1993).

Elaine Roulet

United States, 1930–

Sister of St. Joseph

Prison reform activist

Founder of Providence House, Inc.

"None of us can do anything alone in life."

"Elaine, I'm going to bring you to the rectory."

One day during her frequent colds and earaches, Elaine Roulet was taken to the rectory to be blessed by the priest. After he "delivered the goods," Elaine's mother gave him a dollar, took her daughter, and left for home. Years later, now Sister Elaine commented it was "sad that no one ever told my mother that *she* could have blessed me."

Sister Elaine understood the value of a mother's care and love as it extends to her children. After her father's death while she was still a girl, she saw firsthand her mother working in the Brooklyn Navy Yard, struggling to be a single parent. Perhaps this inspired Elaine's early vision for herself. "I wanted to open up orphanages," she said. "I wanted to do wonderful things." So at age nineteen, she joined the Sisters of St. Joseph and became a teacher and later a school principal.

It seemed as if life had settled into the routine of the school day. The hours were regular, and the commitments long-term. And always there was the endless chatter of children constantly underfoot to encourage and nurture.

One day Sister Elaine was asked to teach reading to the inmates of the Bedford Hills Correctional Facility in Bedford Hills, New York. When she arrived, she discovered there were no programs for the inmates' children. When children visited their mothers twice a week, they were forced to sit across from them at a table behind a barrier. "There was nothing. No books. No food. Nothing." She felt that the children were being punished right along with their mothers.

Sister Elaine made the bureaucratic system realize that sweeping changes had to be made if women were ever to become good mothers and good citizens. They needed to bond with their children, especially their babies. They needed to understand how to parent them, as many had come from abused backgrounds themselves. To help the inmates develop as mothers, Sister Elaine instituted parenting classes, crafts, and job training. She made the prison meeting room look less forbidding and created programs where children could visit their mothers for longer periods or could live nearby.

She rallied volunteers, donors, and public and governmental support in order to change the way women are treated in prison and thus was able to transform older practices into more humane and successful ways of allowing people to improve their own lives. Today these programs have impacted the penal system throughout the nation.

But Sister Elaine is always quick to acknowledge that the job can never be done alone. "I have always received support and help…you can pout alone, you can feel sorry for yourself alone, but you cannot give life alone."

For Further Reading

"Prison Angel," by Joan Gelman, *Rosie Magazine,* January 2002.

Elizabeth Ann Seton

United States, 1774–1821

Wife, mother, convert to Catholicism

Founder of the Sisters of Charity, the nation's first religious community

First native-born saint of the United States

"...teach my heart to find the better way."

Teen-aged Elizabeth Ann Bayley danced and twirled around the grand ballroom in the arms of a well-dressed young gentleman. Her dance card was full, and she was happy to be at such a grand event—a ball in honor of the nation's first president, George Washington. Only those most prominent in society were invited to such occasions. Elizabeth, the daughter of an influential physician, was from one of New York's most respected families. Her days were filled with teas, parties, and balls. Her future would include marriage to the right young man of distinction, and eventually motherhood, and her family would rise in stature and prestige. She knew, she *hoped*, that someday all this would happen.

After courting her for a year, William Seton, heir to an impressive shipping business, married Elizabeth. Their life together produced four children and the home Elizabeth had always dreamed of. But William had inherited the family's disposition toward tuberculosis as well as its fortune. Both his business and his health began to fail. After declaring bankruptcy, he, Elizabeth, and their eldest daughter went to Italy hoping for a cure. It was too late, his illness too advanced, and he died there.

In the span of a decade Elizabeth had gone from having everything to losing everything. She returned to the United States with four children to feed and no money.

While in Italy, she had stayed with a family who introduced her to their Catholic faith. Catholicism provided her with a comfort she continued to seek out when she returned to the United States. But her relatives fiercely opposed her changing religions. Catholicism was looked down upon as the religion of the immigrant rabble. At the invitation of Bishop John Carroll, Elizabeth moved her family to Maryland, where the bishop had invited her to open a school and where she could practice her faith without harassment. In the hills surrounding Emmitsburg, Maryland, she founded a school for girls, the first of what would blossom into the parochial school system in the United States. She also founded the Sisters of Charity, the country's first religious community for women. As their head, she was called Mother Seton. The Sisters of Charity spread out from Emmitsburg to open other schools across the brand new nation.

The education of children, Elizabeth felt, was her special call. "Be children of the Church" was the final instruction she gave to her sisters. Today children across the United States receive the best in educational opportunities supported by the Catholic Church, reaping the benefits of what Mother Seton started some two hundred years ago.

For Further Reading

Elizabeth Ann Seton: Saint for a New Nation by Julie Walters (New York: Paulist Press, 2002).

American Women of Faith by Rawley Myers (Huntington, Ind.: Our Sunday Visitor, 1989).

Mother Maria Skobtsova

Latvia, 1891–1945

Wife, poet, mother, Russian Orthodox religious

Created a new monasticism devoted to social action

Died at Ravensbrück in place of a fellow prisoner

"No amount of thought will ever result in any greater formulation than the three words, 'Love one another....'"

Lisa Skobtsova could not understand how the world had become so disrupted. Holding tight to her small children as they crowded into lines of refugees headed for Paris, she turned over the events of her own past. How foreign it seemed to her present life as an émigré.

Of Russian aristocracy, her family had been able to give her a fine education. Lisa possessed a brilliant mind. She was well known as a poet, became a political activist during the Russian Revolution, and even served as mayor of her hometown. When the revolution became too dangerous, she and her children and her second husband fled. They made the long difficult journey from Anapa, Russia, to Tbilisi, to Istanbul, to Yugoslavia, finally to France and then Paris.

Little Nastia, her precious daughter, died within a few years of their arrival. Shortly after that Lisa separated from her second husband. Through the pain of her daughter's death, she became "aware of a new and special, broad and all-embracing motherhood." Her spirituality, until now largely private and of an academic bent, turned itself outward to direct social action.

Working with impoverished Russian émigrés, she recognized that each person is "the very icon of God incarnate in the world." She gave them maternal compassion and brought to each the feminine face of God. Her work became widely known, and soon the local bishop asked her to become a nun within her own Orthodox tradition. She professed her vows and took the name Mother Maria Skobtsova, but instead of cloistering herself away, she remained in Paris and made the world her monastery.

Mother Maria opened a house of hospitality and welcomed the sick and the homeless, alcoholics and addicts, and those who'd been judged insane. Later, when the Jews sought refuge from the Nazis, she sheltered them too and helped them escape. But her social action was always informed by the gospel message. Every charitable action had to be performed with meaning and love; there was no other way to heaven. She said, "About every poor, hungry and imprisoned person the Savior says 'I': 'I was hungry and thirsty, I was sick and in prison.' ...[H]e puts an equal sign between himself and anyone in need...."

In 1940, the Nazis entered Paris and demanded that Mother Maria stop helping Jews. She refused. She was arrested and transported to Germany to the death camp Ravensbrück. She remained there for two years. In the final days of the camps, Jews were killed hurriedly in order to get rid of as many as possible. Only days away from being liberated by Russian troops, Mother Maria died in the gas chamber. Although the exact details of her death are not known, it is said that she stepped into the line for the gas chamber to take the place of a Jew. A fellow inmate who survived the camps memorized her final words to the world: "I completely accept suffering in the knowledge that this is how things ought to be for me, and if I am to die, I see this as a blessing from on high."

For Further Reading

Mother Maria Skobtsova: Essential Writings, edited by Jim Forest (Maryknoll, N.Y.: Orbis Books, 2002).

Pearl of Great Price by Father Sergei Hackel (Crestwood, N.Y.: St.Vladimir's Seminary Press, 1981).

The Ladder of the Beatitudes by Jim Forest (Maryknoll, N.Y.: Orbis Books, 1999).

Edith Stein

Germany, 1891–1942

Converted to Catholicism; became a Carmelite religious

Writer, philosopher, intellectual

Died in Auschwitz due to her Jewish heritage

Martyr for both Jews and Catholics

"Those who seek the truth seek God, whether they realize it or not."

Having read through the night, Edith Stein at last closed the cover and put the book on the table. The book was the autobiography of a Carmelite nun named Teresa of Avila, written four hundred years ago. It had so moved Edith that she knew instinctively it would change her life. She'd always had the greatest conviction that she was to have a profound destiny. Could this book be the way?

It was strange that a brilliant, twentieth-century Jewish atheist studying philosophy at Germany's University of Gottingen should be attracted to a sixteenth-century nun. But the Carmelite way of living made sense and seemed to have the answer to so many questions Edith had struggled with. Within months, she converted to Catholicism and ultimately would enter the Carmelite convent.

Edith's pious mother was devastated and remained so until the day she died. It was unthinkable that her daughter had become an atheist, then a Catholic, then a nun as well. But Edith neither left her Jewish roots behind nor used her Catholic faith to hide from what was happening to the Jews in Nazi Germany. Seeking an audience with Pope Pius XI, she wanted to ask for the church's involvement in protecting the Jews. Her request for an audience was turned down.

More than a decade after converting, Edith joined the Carmelite convent at Cologne, Germany, in 1934, and took the name of Teresa Benedicta of the Cross. Though cloistered, she and her superiors were aware of political events outside the convent. As a former Jew, Edith might be in danger. Her presence might also endanger her fellow sisters. She left Germany and traveled to another Carmelite convent at Echt, in the Netherlands. At both convents, she was encouraged to pursue her philosophical writing.

In her work she returned again and again to the image of the cross, especially in her final years. Suffering, in particular the current suffering of the Jews, could be united with Christ's on the cross. "The Savior is not alone on the Cross," she wrote. Everyone who suffered patiently and freely for Christ's sake helped to lighten his burden and also united more closely with him. "The suffering of reparation, accepted freely, is what joins us most of all to the Lord." As a Jew turned Catholic, she felt herself especially called to be wed to the cross.

In 1940, the Nazis occupied the Netherlands and forced all Jews, even those who had converted, to wear the Yellow

Star of David. Two years after that, the Catholic bishops of Holland wrote a pastoral letter denouncing the Nazi system. Almost immediately soldiers were sent throughout the Netherlands to arrest any and all Jews who had turned Christian. Edith and her sister Rosa, who had also converted, were taken along with fifteen hundred others to Auschwitz. Within the first two weeks, they were both killed in the gas chambers.

Edith Stein leaves a remarkable legacy. The papers that she wrote on scholarly subjects have yet to be fully appreciated and await a new generation of thinkers. In her, Catholicism is reunited with its Jewish roots. She is a shared martyr, stretching out her hands to both religions.

For Further Reading

"Edith Stein: The Prescience of God," in *A Passion for Life: Fragments of the Face of God* by Joan Chittister (Maryknoll, N.Y.: Orbis Press, 1996).

Saint Edith Stein: Blessed by the Cross by Mary Lea Hill (Boston: Pauline Books & Media, 1999).

Kateri Tekakwitha

United States, 1656–1680

*Native American, called
"The Lily of the Mohawks"*

Mystic, convert to Catholicism

"Like a lily among thorns...."

Four-year old Kateri lay awake listening to the sounds of weeping around her. Her younger brother and mother had just died. Her father, chief of the Turtle Clan, had died only a few days before. Now she was alone. Her eyes burned and she could not see her small hand as she held it in front of her face. What would become of her? Who would take care of her? Would she ever be able to see again?

Introduced by European settlers, a smallpox epidemic raged through North America during the 1600s and killed over 20,000 Native Americans. As a result of her own case of smallpox, Kateri would live her entire life with a scarred face and minimal vision. She formed the habit of holding a veil over her eyes to protect them from strong sun rays.

After her parents died, Kateri went to live with her uncle and aunt and helped them with the daily work of grinding corn, planting the fields, and tending the harvest. She never complained and found comfort thinking about the tiny fragments she remembered about her mother's religion—Christianity.

Kateri worked hard to become part of her uncle's Mohawk community. Even though she did not always participate in their religious rituals, she wanted to be a part of their life, as they were a part of hers. But a different community awaited her. Having a Christian mother prepared her for meeting the Jesuits when they came to her village. From the beginning she felt connected to the Jesuits, while the other Mohawks were suspicious and fearful of their new ideas.

Kateri was overcome with love and devotion to Jesus. The idea of Jesus as the suffering servant matched perfectly her idea of her own life and changed her forever. She also refused to marry, but sought to remain a virgin.

This dangerous move quickly led to additional suffering as she was ostracized even more from the Mohawks. Preserving the family unit meant tradition and survival, so the Mohawks believed she was turning her back on them. Additionally, her preference for the white man's religion was an offense. The whites were the reason for disease and starvation.

Once Kateri was baptized by the Jesuits into the Catholic faith, her life became a daily crucifixion. Her refusal to accept marriage proposals led to repeated stonings, harassment, and other abuse. Through it all, she practiced her faith devoutly, feeling her heart was with God's and that she would be protected.

Eventually not even her uncle's house could provide safety for her. A Jesuit priest living with the tribe realized she'd soon be killed if she stayed with the Mohawks. He arranged for her to be taken to a location in Canada where there were other Native American Christians.

Kateri's spiritual life took flight once she was free to practice her religion without fear. She fasted, spent hours in prayer before the altar, and performed small acts of charity. In a time when whites viewed the Native American as savage, Kateri startled them with her devotion, love for God, and obvious holiness. In time, even the Mohawks came to admire and respect her strength of commitment, and upon her death at twenty-four, many of them converted.

For Further Reading

Kateri Tekakwitha, Mohawk Maid by Evelyn M. Brown (New York: Farrar, Straus & Company, 1958).

"Kateri Tekakwitha, Icon of Otherness," from *A Passion for Life: Fragments of the Face of God* by Joan D. Chittister (Maryknoll, N.Y.: Orbis Press, 1996).

Kateri of the Mohawks by Marie Cecilia Buehrle (Milwaukee: Bruce Publishing, 1954).

Mother Teresa

Yugoslavia, 1910–1997

Sister of Loreto; founder of the Missionaries of Charity

Writer, international speaker, and activist for the poor

Recipient of the Nobel Prize for Peace

"I am a little pencil in the hands of God."

Young Agnes listened intently to a letter being read from a missionary priest living in India. India was a strange faraway land filled with hungry people, homeless people, suffering people. Agnes wanted to help. She knew deep inside that she could do it; she could help those people, but how and when? And, more importantly, was this God's way?

Her mother had always told her to trust in Jesus so completely, it was like putting your hand in his. So that was what Agnes did. She knew that once you hold someone else's hand, you lessen your own fear and are never alone.

At eighteen, Agnes left her home and family in Albania and crossed Europe to Ireland, where she entered the convent of the Sisters of Loreto. There she took the name Maria Teresa of the Child Jesus. By the end of the year she left Ireland for India.

While there, she did not help the poor right away. First she had to finish her religious training, which continued for nine years; most of these years she spent as a teacher. At that point she was made principal of St. Mary's School, where she taught history and geography. The girls at the school called her Mother. She thought she was happy, but deep inside a small voice was becoming louder. She realized that she was not doing what she had come to India to do. She enjoyed teaching the school's middle-class children, but a larger, needier group waited for her right outside the school building. She wanted to care for those poor people whom she'd heard about so long ago, the poor people she now saw everyday lying in the streets. This is what she felt she had been called to do all along.

The bishop and sisters at the school were worried by what Mother Teresa was proposing to them. She wanted to leave the convent and live on the streets with the poor. How would she survive? How would she take care of herself? She would be making herself the same as anyone else living in the streets, just one more homeless person. But that was precisely the point. Mother Teresa felt that God wanted her "to be poor with the poor and to love him in the distressing disguise of the poorest of the poor."

She left the convent, taking nothing with her but the certainty of her call. She began to care for the sick and the homeless, for those who died in the street because they had no place else to go. Soon some of the girls from the school visited her. Many stayed because they felt called to live with the poor as well. A Rule was written to help focus their goals. The sisters called themselves the Missionaries of Charity. Suddenly others began to recognize the poor on the streets when they saw them through the eyes of Mother Teresa.

In time, Mother Teresa's work was recognized and spread beyond Calcutta to other countries. She won numerous awards, including the Nobel Peace Prize, the Pope John XXIII Prize for peace, and the Albert Schweitzer International Prize. She saw all these good things as only a drop in the ocean of the world's suffering. "Today it is fashionable to talk about the poor. Unfortunately it is not fashionable to talk with them," she said. "The poor are Christ Himself....When we touch the sick and needy, we touch the suffering body of Christ."

For Further Reading

Mother Teresa: A Life of Love by Elaine Murray Stone (New York: Paulist Press, 1999).

Mother Teresa: A Complete Authorized Biography by Kathryn Spink (San Francisco: Harper San Francisco, 1998).

LOVE: A Fruit Always in Season, Daily Meditations by Mother Teresa, edited by Dorothy S. Hunt (San Francisco: Ignatius Press, 1987).

Teresa of Avila

Spain, 1515–1582

Mystic, writer, reformer of the Carmelite order

Author of *The Interior Castle*, a classic on prayer

First woman doctor of the church

"In every little thing created by God there is more than we realize, even in so small a thing as a tiny ant."

Little Teresa talked her older brother into running away from their home in Avila, Spain. They headed toward the town where they thought the Moors, who had been at war with the Spanish, would capture them and take them prisoner. "I want to see God," Teresa had told her brother. "Maybe they will cut off our heads!" Fortunately for both children, their desire for a dramatic martyrdom was thwarted when their uncle met them on the bridge that led into town and promptly sent them home.

As a young woman, Teresa was torn between her love of life and her concern for her soul. She enjoyed the comfortable lifestyle her wealthy father provided for his family, but it was not enough. She became convinced that she should enter the convent. Her father would not give his consent, so she ran away. Her father loved his headstrong daughter very much and eventually gave his blessing. But after Teresa entered the convent, she fell ill. Fainting spells and heart problems placed her on bed rest. Finally, she was ordered to leave the convent and go to her sister's house in the country.

During this time of trial, Teresa found her prayer life expanding. Once she was well, she went back to the convent on fire with the new ideas she had discovered in her prayer life. But these ideas became threatening to others. She was ostracized by her fellow nuns and questioned by the church. It was the time of the Inquisition, a dangerous period for anyone, especially women, who favored change. Were her ideas really inspired by God, or by the devil? Her experiences were intensely mystical, yet she herself was charming, outgoing, and witty, an unsettling combination.

Teresa's books were examined by church authorities. She ran the risk of being burned at the stake as had been done to countless others, but she was ultimately cleared by the Inquisition. Then she put her ideas into action and traveled across Spain reforming her order of nuns, reminding them to practice their ideals of charity and poverty. Though her work was difficult, Teresa knew that this was what she'd been called to do.

Canonized a saint in 1622, in 1970 Teresa of Avila was raised to the position of a doctor of the church. This means that her teaching, especially her teaching on prayer, is to be regarded as coming directly from the Holy Spirit. She was the first woman to be made a doctor of the church.

For Further Reading

"Teresa of Avila: Face of Fire," in *A Passion for Life* by Joan Chittister (Maryknoll, N.Y.: Orbis Press, 1996).

A Year with the Saints: Quotations and Extracts for Every Day of the Year by Mark Water (Liguori, Mo.: Liguori Publications, 1997).

Life of Saint Teresa of Avila by Herself, translated and with an introduction by J. M. Cohen (New York: Penguin Books, 1988).

Thérèse of Lisieux

France, 1873–1897

Carmelite religious, mystic, writer

Author of *Story of a Soul,* her autobiography

Doctor of the church for her "little way" to God

"A small spark, O mystery of life, is enough to start an immense fire."

Young Thérèse Martin couldn't help but feel abandoned once more, watching her older sister, Marie, walk down the road that led to town. At the end of the road, Marie would enter a convent belonging to the Carmelites, an order that had been reformed by the Spanish nun Teresa of Avila.

Today this convent would hold two of Thérèse's sisters; a convent of the Poor Clares held a third sister. Each in turn had been a mother to Thérèse since their own mother's death in 1877. The house where she lived with her father and last sister, Celine, was becoming empty.

But Thérèse held a secret deep in her heart, a secret she had shared only with her sister Pauline. Thérèse, too, wished to be admitted to the religious life at Carmel. Someday, she hoped, there would be four Martin sisters living in the Carmelite convent of Lisieux!

Never known for patience, Thérèse had been the spoiled baby of the family. She was prone to tears and did not let anything stand in the way of what she wanted. Once realizing she had a religious vocation, she set about gaining approval in the same headstrong way. She sought not only her father's and her uncle's permission to enter early, but she sought the pope's as well when the local bishop showed reluctance due to her age.

Girls of fourteen were considered too young to make such a lifelong commitment. How could they know, at that age, whether they were truly willing to give up forever a husband and children, parties, travel, and all the material things of society? But Thérèse felt a sureness and a love for Jesus that gave her a deep commitment. During a family vacation in Italy to see Pope Leo XIII, she grabbed him around the knees as she knelt before him and begged to be admitted to the convent. But not even this display of fervor was able to bring about her request, and she was forced to wait.

A year later, at the age of fifteen, Thérèse finally entered the walls of Carmel. She felt that pride was her special weakness due to her many gifts, so she began rooting out any form of self-admiration. She knew she would never accomplish great deeds and instead practiced what she called a "little way." She described it as "the way of spiritual childhood, the way of trust and absolute self-surrender."

Thérèse's little way consisted of acts of simple love that were so tiny they went unnoticed in the routine of daily life. She went out of her way to help with the many chores around the convent that others would prefer not to do. She made it her job to interact with the most difficult people, the ones whom others might avoid. And she would hasten to do the jobs that others might find distasteful or beneath them.

Thérèse never wavered from her knowledge that this little way of doing things was what Jesus expected of her. Her calling from him seemed clear—to show love and charity to everyone in every way. She took to thinking of herself as growing smaller and insignificant, but the reality was the opposite. She also performed many acts of charity and love for those outside the Carmel convent. She prayed for prisoners in jail facing death. She prayed for missionaries and wanted to become one. She prayed for priests as a special spiritual partner in their ministry.

Thérèse died at the young age of twenty-four. She had made herself so unremarkable that after her death, another nun said that there was nothing to say about her. Shortly afterward, her brief collection of writings came to be known, and many miracles were performed through her intercession. In just a few years, the church officially granted what she had wanted so earnestly during her life: sainthood. Not only that, but her path to heaven through her little way was considered so true, so important, that she was made a doctor of the church in 1997. Through her "little way," Thérèse showed that there is holiness in ordinary life and that simple, everyday love can be transforming when grounded in faith.

For Further Reading

The Story of a Life: St. Thérèse of Lisieux by Guy Gaucher (New York: Harper and Row, 1987).

Thérèse: Saint of a Little Way by Frances Parkinson Keyes (New York: Julian Messner, 1937).

Autobiography of St. Thérèse of Lisieux, translated by Ronald Knox (New York: P. J. Kenedy and Sons, 1957).

Sojourner Truth

United States, 1797–1883

Wife, mother, ex-slave,
itinerant preacher

Anti-slavery activist and
promoter of women's rights

Acclaimed as the most influential
woman of her day

"And did not the same Savior die
to save the one as well as the other?"

Nine-year-old Isabella stood alone as the slave auctioneer repeated the dollar amounts yelled out by the audience. It was noisy and hot, and there had been lots of activity among the buyers when she stood up on the stage. When she heard the words "one hundred dollars," spray from the auctioneer's mouth hit the back of her head. The sale was over. She had been sold to a man by the name of John Nealy of Ulster County, New York. She watched the faces of her loving parents fade into the crowd of people swarming to take charge of her. Her parents had been lucky with Isabella. They had had her to themselves for nine years while her other brothers and sisters had been either sold or stolen long before the age of two.

Great Women of Faith

Looking at her new master, she felt he would provide her a good home. His face looked kind, and that was a bonus. But the tiny pride she felt over the high price he'd paid for her quickly faded into shame as she realized that she'd been bought along with a group of sheep. The new master had been more interested in their well-being than her own.

As a young woman, Isabella was given in a slave marriage ceremony to a man named Thomas, for whom she bore five children. When one of her children was sold illegally into slavery outside the state, she sued for his return after contacting a group that she was told would help her—the Society of Friends.

One day, placing her youngest child on one hip and all she owned in a sack on the other, she walked off the master's farm to her freedom. She found her way to New York City, where she worked as a cook, maid, and laundress. In 1843, at the age of forty-six, she felt called to a new life, one of combating slavery with the gospel message. She changed her name to Sojourner Truth and became an itinerant preacher on the issues of slavery and women's rights, which she felt were strongly linked. With the abolitionist movement centered in the North, the great speakers of the age—William Lloyd Garrison, Lucretia Mott, and Susan B. Anthony—were soon her friends.

In 1850 she dictated the story of her life to a friend, for she herself could neither read nor write. *The Narrative of Sojourner Truth* was written down by Olive Gilbert and became one of the first accounts of the horrors of slavery and the African American experience. Sojourner traveled the east coast and Midwest, selling her book and portraits in order to make money for her cause. She became a highly sought-after speaker known for her wit, straightforward thinking, and vocal talents.

Sojourner eventually ended up in Battle Creek, Michigan, where she bought a house in a place called Harmonia. From Michigan, she became involved in the Civil War, helping black troops. She was invited to the White House to dine with Abraham Lincoln and continued working for equal rights for all until her death. She was not intimidated by anyone as she traveled the country speaking out boldly. Responding to the argument that the Bible said women were inferior, she quipped, "And how came Jesus into the world? Through God who created him and the woman who bore him. Man, where was your part?"

For Further Reading

Narrative of Sojourner Truth (1850) by Sojourner Truth with Olive Gilbert (Mineola, N.Y.: Dover Publications, 1997).

$\mathcal{S}$imone $\mathcal{W}$eil

France, 1909–1943

Teacher, philosopher, activist for human rights, writer

Died in England from malnutrition in solidarity with the suffering of war-torn France

"If we turn our mind toward the good, it is impossible that little by little the whole soul will not be attracted thereto in spite of itself."

Little Simone knew nothing but fighting all her life. A frail, sickly child, she moved with her brother and Jewish parents from one military area to another around France. Her father, a physician, had been mobilized by the army as it entered the First World War. As he tended the sick and maimed, Simone attended school and excelled in her class work. She was a deep thinker. She wanted answers to the most important questions she saw being ignored around her. Why was there such poverty? Why didn't everyone have the same advantages in life? Why was life unfair?

She entered the field of philosophy. From 1925 to 1928 she attended the Lycee Henri IV in France, where she studied with the famous philosopher Emile-Auguste Chartier. From this point on, pursuing questions and struggling between different answers would consume her life.

Soon after graduation, she began to teach. But instead of dwelling solely in the academic world, merely debating issues, Simone set out to experience them. To live out her philosophical ideas, she also took manual labor jobs. She joined an assembly line in a factory but found she wasn't strong enough. She worked in a vineyard to learn how people survived on such meager wages. She also participated in protests for workers rights and often gave her own money to unemployed workers. Due to her political ideas and activities, she was let go from several teaching jobs. But she never thought twice about what she was doing. Solidarity with the poor, the under-served, and the underprivileged was what she strove to achieve.

This idea of solidarity with others led her to become involved in the Spanish Civil War. But the war's brutal consequences on children, the elderly, women, and society at large disillusioned her and resulted in a major shift in her thinking. She renounced being a pacifist, saying that nonviolent protest could not stop violent action. From 1934 on, she struggled with the concepts of peace, protest, and human rights versus the merits of a just war.

It was at this time that she was drawn to Christianity. The ideals of Jesus excited her and, while visiting a Benedictine abbey in 1938, she had a mystical experience of Christ's Passion entering her soul. While her writings are often grounded in politics and the material circumstances of life caused by suffering, this experience gave her an indelible sense of the nearness of God: "We must feel the reality and presence of God through all external things, without exception, as clearly as our hand feels the substance of paper through the penholder and the nib."

From then on she considered herself Christian yet she was never baptized, unwilling to let baptism separate her from the world's unbelievers. "...[N]othing gives me more pain than the idea of separating myself from the immense and unfortunate multitude of unbelievers. I have the essential need, and I think I can say the vocation, to move among men of every class and complexion, mixing with them and sharing their life...."

World War II came to the doorstep of her parents' home in France. When Paris fell to the Nazis in 1940, she fled with her Jewish family to the United States rather than risk internment in a concentration camp. She later returned to England, where she worked for the Free French organization until she collapsed at her desk, weak with tuberculosis. In the English hospital, to join in solidarity with the people of France, she ate only the normal ration given to the average man, woman, and child in France suffering under the occupation. It was not enough in her weakened condition, and she died at the age of thirty-four.

Simone Weil's writings are currently held as some of the greatest works in peace and justice this century has seen. She lived the way she thought, fighting to transform the world at war with itself.

For Further Reading

Waiting for God by Simone Weil (New York: Harper Perennial, 2001).

Spiritual Guides for Today by Annice Callahan, R.S.C.J. (New York: Crossroad, 1992).

"Simone Weil: Icon of the Face of Truth," in *A Passion for Life: Fragments of the Face of God* by Joan Chittister (Maryknoll, N.Y.: Orbis Books, 2000).

ℒois 𝒲ilson

United States, 1891–1988

Wife, teacher, artist

Cofounder of Al-Anon,
a program that supports families
and friends of alcoholics

*"I believe that people are good if you give them
half a chance and that good is more
powerful than evil."*

The first summer Lois Burnham met Bill Wilson, she didn't
give him much thought. Like her, Bill was just another person
who came to spend summers in the hills of rural Vermont.
Lois's father, a surgeon and gynecologist, had brought his family there for several years. Lois found nothing unusual in Bill
Wilson, never imagining he'd eventually be her husband.

After several more summers, Bill and Lois married in
1918, just before he shipped out to Europe to fight in the First
World War. Before this, with an educational background in
art, she had worked in New Jersey in her aunt's school. After
Bill left, Lois worked as an occupational therapist. When the
war ended in 1919 and Bill returned, she was eager to settle

down and begin their family, buy a house, and build a future together.

A series of miscarriages made it impossible for the young couple to have children of their own. They then tried to adopt but were not accepted by the agencies whenever they were investigated. Lois could not figure out why. How could a young couple with educational backgrounds as strong as theirs, and with a potential for good income, be turned down repeatedly? Other couples not half as well off were being approved.

The answer was finally revealed to her. It was Bill's heavy drinking. Lois began to learn just how bad it was. First she heard stories from his army buddies and realized his drinking had gotten worse during the war and afterward. Soon she saw the effects of it firsthand. Because of alcohol, Bill couldn't complete his studies and had to leave law school. Then his brief career as an advisor to Wall Street brokerage firms also fell apart. People began to avoid him, and Lois became very worried that they had no future.

At last with no place left to live, the Wilsons began to move from one friend's house to the next, accepting whatever hospitality was offered them, while Lois worked at various jobs. Though she was desperate to help her husband, she at last realized that even though she had the skills to help others, Bill needed to help himself. There was nothing she could do.

Bill eventually found healing for his alcoholism and went on to cofound Alcoholics Anonymous to help others. Lois was to reach out to their families through her own experience. She cofounded the Al-Anon Family Groups, a community resource providing support to families and friends affected by an alcoholic's drinking. Today there are over 26,000 Al-Anon and

Alateen groups that meet in 115 countries around the world. Lois turned her own pain into a legacy of caring and commitment to others.

For Further Reading

Lois Remembers: Memoirs of the Co-Founder of Al-Anon and Wife of the Co-Founder of Alcoholics Anonymous by Lois Wilson (Virginia Beach: Al-Anon Family Group, 1979).

Additional References**

** Please note: All Web-site references were current at the time of writing. However, as site maintenance can lapse and as sites change servers, particular page addresses may change. If any site does not currently link, go to a search engine such as Google (www.google.com) or Alta Vista (www.altavista.com), and enter the woman's name. On a separate query, also enter any organizations mentioned in the reference.

Jane Addams

1. Quote is from the Web site for the San Antonio Peace Center: www.salsa.net/peace/quotes/html.
2. National-Louis University Web site on Jane Addams: http://www.nl.edu/ace/Resources/Addams.html.
3. University of Chicago at Illinois Website: http://www.uic.edu/jaddams/hull/ja_bio.html.

Josephine Bakhita

1. Opening and final quotes are from the Web site of the National Black Catholic Congress: http://www.nbccongress.org/facts/josephine.htm.
   The middle quote about tattooing is from the Web site of the Catholic Community Forum: http://www.catholic-forum.com/saints/saintj84.htm.
3. Web site of the Holy Angels African American Catholic Church in Chicago: http://www.holyangels.com/SaintGuiseppineJosephineBakhita.htm.

Thea Bowman

1. Initial quote is from *Families: Black and Catholic, Catholic and Black* (Wash., D.C.: United States Conference of Catholic Bishops, 1985).
2. Interior quotes are from the video *Sister Thea: Her Own Story* (St. Louis: Oblate Media and Communications Corp., 1991).

Mother Frances Cabrini

1. All quotes are from Myers, pages 54 and 62.
2. The Web site of the Mother Cabrini Shrine: http://www.den-cabrini-shrine.org/.
3. The Web site of the Missionary Sisters of the Sacred Heart of Jesus: http://www.mothercabrini.com/.

Agneta Chang

1. Quote is from Ellsberg, pages 430–31.
2. Maryknoll Mission Archives, Maryknoll Sisters, Maryknoll, New York.
3. "Korea's Gift to Mission," by Bernice Kita, M.M., *Maryknoll Magazine,* November 2000, posted at the Maryknoll Web site: http://www.maryknoll.org/MEDIA/xMAGAZINE/xmag2000/xmag11/m11s7.htm.

Frances Crowe

1. Initial and interior quotes are from True, pages 37–38.
2. "Nonviolent Resistance to Raytheon's Lethal Commerce," cited on: http://leb.net/~bcome/activism/raytheon-vigil.html.
3. "Profiles: Frances Crowe," a 1999 interview by Mark K. Anderson in *The Valley Advocate,* posted on its Web site: http://www.valleyadvocate.com/bestof99valley/pro6.html.

4. "A Brief History of Northampton," on Northampton, Massachusetts' Web site: http://www.noho.com/townhistory.html.

Dorothy Day

1. Quotes are from *Meditations by Dorothy Day,* selected and arranged by Stanley Vishnewski (New York: Paulist Press, 1970), pages 7, 92, and 47.
2. *Praying with Dorothy Day* by James Allaire and Rosemary Broughton (Winona, Minn.: St. Mary's Press, 1995).
3. "An Appetite for God: Dorothy Day at 100," by Patrick Jordan, *Commonweal,* October 24, 1997.

Catherine de Hueck Doherty

1. Initial and end quotes are from the Catherine Doherty Cause for Canonization Web site: http://www.madonnahouse.org/mandate/index.html and http://www.catherinedoherty.org/life/index.html. Interior quotes are from *Molchanie*, pages 11 and 65.
2. Web site for Madonna House: http://madonnahouse.org.

Mother Katharine Drexel

1. Initial quote is from Rawley, page 98; interior quote is from the Web site of the Sisters of the Blessed Sacrament: http://www.katharinedrexel.org/vocation.htm.
2. Main Web site of the Sisters of the Blessed Sacrament: http://www.katharinedrexel.org/.
3. "Katharine Drexel" on the Web site of the Catholic Community Forum: http://www.catholic-forum.com/saints/saintk03.htm.

Maria Faustina

1. Quote is from Sister Faustina's diary (163), cited on the Saint Faustina Web site:
   http://www.faustina.ch/index_en.htm.
2. The Divine Mercy pages on the Web site of the Marians of the Immaculate Conception:
   http://www.marian.org/divinemercy/index.html.

Maria Goretti

1. Quote is from "The Trinitarian Interior Life of St. Maria Goretti," by James Likoudis on the Friends of Maria Goretti Web site: http://www.mariagoretti.org/LikoudisArticle.html.
2. "St. Maria Goretti and her Murderer, Allesandro," by James Likoudis, posted on the Friends of Maria Goretti Web site: http://www.mariagoretti.org/LikoudisArticle2.html.

José Hobday

1. Initial quote is from the *You Chose Well* audiotape; interior quotes are from *Stories of Awe and Abundance*, page 15.
2. *Simple Living: The Path to Joy and Freedom* by Sister José Hobday, O.S.F. (New York: Continuum, 1998).
3. Phone interview with José Hobday by the author on January 24, 2002.

Juana Inés de la Cruz

1. Initial quote is from Cahill, page 111; the second is from "The Poetry of Sor Juana Inés de la Cruz," "Disillusionment," translated by Alan Trueblood, posted at:
   http://www.sappho.com/poetry/historical/j_ines.html.
2. The Juana Inés de la Cruz Project sponsored by Dartmouth College: http://www.dartmouth.edu/~sorjuana/.

3. The Juana Inés de la Cruz site maintained by the Women's Studies Department at the University of Arizona, posted at: http://w3.arizona.edu/~ws/ws200/fall97/grp10/grp10.htm

Chiara Lubich

1. Initial quote is from the Focalare Web site: www.rc.net/focolare; the interior quote from Zanbonini, page 82.

Mary MacKillop

1. Quote is from Gardiner, page 449.
2. Web site of the Sisters of Saint Joseph of the Sacred Heart (the Josephites): http://www.sosj.org.au/.
3. Flinders Ranges Research, historical research site of southern Australia:
   http://members.ozemail.com.au/~fliranre/mackillop.htm.

Raïssa Maritain

1. Initial quote is from Suther, page 12; interior quotes are from *We Have Been Friends Together* by Raïssa Maritain (New York: Longmans, Green and Co., 1942), pages 63–64, and *Raïssa's Journal,* page 87; end quote is from *We Have Been Friends Together,* page 158.
2. "Raïssa Maritain: Philosopher, Poet, Mystic," by Michael Sherwin, O.P., on the Web site for the Catholic Educator's Resource Center:
   http://catholiceducation.org/articles/arts/al0052. html#footnote20.
3. "Raïssa Maritain," article on the Christian Mystics site at: http://www.christianmystics.com/articles/womenmystics/ raissamaritain.shtml.

Ƶelie Martin

1. Both quotes from Gaucher, page 11.
2. "Louis Martin and Zelie Guerin," on the Web site of the Carmelite Province of the Most Pure Heart of Mary: http://carmelnet.org/sword/v60/Spirituality/sp-martins/sp-martins.htm.
3. Web site of the Society of the Little Flower: http://www.littleflower.org/therese/story_parents.html.
4. "Thérèse of Lisieux, Doctor of the Church," by John W. Donohue, *America,* December, 1997.

Mary of the Incarnation

1. Initial quote is from Sirach 26:16; interior quote from the Saints Alive Web site: http://www.stthomasirondequoit.com/SaintsAlive/id274.htm.
2. "Blessed Marie de l' Incarnation," at the New Advent *Catholic Encyclopedia* Web page: http://www.newadvent.org/cathen/09667b.htm.
3. "Marie of the Incarnation" at the Web site of the Catholic Community Forum: http://www.catholic-forum.com/saints/saintm39.htm.

Flannery O'Connor

1. Initial quote is from *Mystery and Manners*, page 159; the second quote, page 167; the final quote is from "A Good Writer Is Hard to Find," by Ronald Weber, *Catholic Dossier* 5, no. 4 (July-August 1999), pages 30–32, posted online at: http://catholiceducation.org/articles/arts/al0041.html.
2. The Flannery O'Connor Web site maintained by the Georgia College and State University: http://library.gcsu.edu/~sc/foc.html.

Maura O'Halloran

1. All quotes are from O'Halloran's journal, pages 20, 15, and 142. The Merton quote is from *Thoughts on the East* by Thomas Merton (New York: New Directions, 1995), page 30.

Rosa Parks

1. Initial and end quotes are from Parks and Reed, page 84 and page 17; interior quote from Parks's mother is from the Hall of Public Service site at: http://www.achievement.org/autodoc/page/parObio-!.

Helen Prejean

1. Quote is from the article "Sympathy for the Devil," by Marc Bruno, on the Salon Web page: http://www.salon.com/06/reviews/dead3.html.

Mollie Rogers

1. All quotations are from "The Spirituality of Mollie Rogers," by Elizabeth E. Carr, from *Feminist Voices in Spirituality*, edited by Pierre Hegy (Lewiston, N.Y.: Edwin Mellen Press, 1996).
2. *Maryknoll's First Lady* by Sister Jeanne Marie Lyons (Archives of the Maryknoll Sisters, Maryknoll, N.Y.).
3. *To the Uttermost Parts of the Earth: The Spirit and Charism of Mary Josephine Rogers* by Sister Camilla Kennedy. (Archives of the Maryknoll Sisters, Maryknoll, N.Y.).

Elaine Roulet

1. All quotes are from the Gelman article and from a luncheon address by Sister Elaine Roulet at "Voices and Visions: The Family and Corrections," proceedings of the First National

Conference on the Family and Corrections, April 24–27, 1988, Sacramento, Calif., cited at: http://www.fcnetwork.org/1stconf/fmcorcon1.html#roulet.

Mother Seton

1 Quotes are from *Elizabeth Bayley Seton* by Elaine Murray Stone (New York: Paulist Press, 1993), and from "St. Elizabeth Ann Seton," from the New Advent *Catholic Encyclopedia,* Web site: http://www.newadvent.org/cathen/13739a.htm.
2. Home page of the Seton National Shrine: www.setonshrine.org.

Mother Maria Skobtsova

1. All quotes are from "Mother Maria Skobtsova: Nun and Martyr" by Jim Forrest, posted on In Communion, the Web site of the Orthodox Peace Fellowship: http://www.incommunion.org/resources/skobtsova.asp.
2. "Mother Maria Skobtsova: Woman of Many Faces, Mother in Many Ways" by Father Michael Plekon in *Jacob's Well*, Fall-Winter, 1999–2000, a publication of the Orthodox Church in America, posted online at: http://www.jacwell.org/Fall_Winter99/Plekon_Mother_Maria.htm.

Edith Stein

1. Initial quote is from "Edith Stein: A Fragmented Life" by Steven Payne, *America*, October 10, 1998, posted on the magazine's Web site : http://www.americapress.org/articles/Payne.htm. Second quote is from the Edith Stein Index, maintained online by the Discalced Carmelite Order: http://www.ocd.pcn.net/ed_en2.htm.

Kateri Tekakwitha

1. Initial quote is from the Song of Solomon 2:2.

Mother Teresa

1. Initial quote is from Hunt, page 243; second quote is from Stone, page 5; final quote is from the Mother Teresa Web site: http://www.tisv.be/mt/quot.htm.
2. *Mother Teresa: The Early Years* by David Porter (Grand Rapids: Eerdmans, 1986).

Teresa of Avila

1. First two quotes are from Chittister, page 78; the third quote is from *St. Teresa of Avila* by Giorgio Papasogli (Boston: Pauline Books & Media, 1992), pages 27–28.
2. *Doctors of the Church: Thirty-Three Men and Women Who Shaped Christianity* by Bernard McGinn (New York: Crossroad, 1999).

Thérèse of Lisieux

1. Initial quote is from Gaucher, page 207; the second is from "St. Thérèse: 1897–1997," on the EWTN Web site: http://www.ewtn.com/therese/therese5.htm.
2. Web site of the Society of the Little Flower: http://littleflower.org/.

Sojourner Truth

1. Both quotes are from speeches given by Sojourner Truth and reprinted in newspapers of the time, posted at the Web site of the Sojourner Truth Institute:

http://www.sojournertruth.org/Library/Speeches/Default.
htm#RIGHTS.
2. Sojourner Truth's speeches on the Text Library at:
   http://www.unl.edu/legacy/19cwww/books/elibe/truth/home.htm.

Simone Weil

1. Initial quote is from *Gravity and Grace* by Simone Weil (New York: Routledge, 1992), page 106; second and end quotes are from *Waiting for God,* pages 3–4 and page 6.

Lois Wilson

1. Initial quote is from the Web site of Stepping Stones, Lois and Bill Wilson's house and now a museum:
   http://www.steppingstones.org/LoisStory.ivnu.

DATE DUE			
4-28			